Never Don't PAY ATTENTION

The Life of Rodeo Photographer Louise L. Serpa

Jan Cleere

Jan Cleere

TWODOT®

GUILFORD, CONNECTICUT
HELENA, MONTANA

A · TWODOT® · BOOK

An imprint and registered trademark of Rowman & Littlefield

Distributed by NATIONAL BOOK NETWORK

British Library Cataloguing in Publication Information Available

Library of Congress Cataloging-in-Publication Data

Cleere, Jan.
Never don't pay attention : the life of rodeo photographer Louise
   L. Serpa / Jan Cleere.
      pages cm
Includes bibliographical references and index.
ISBN 978-1-4422-4727-7 (pbk. : alk. paper)—ISBN 978-1-4422-4728-4 (electronic)
1. Serpa, Louise L. (Louise Larocque) 2. Women photographers—United States. 3. Photography—United States. 4. Photography—West (U.S.) 5. Rodeos—United States—Pictorial works. 6. Cowboys—United States—Pictorial works. I. Title.
GV1834.5.C54 2015
770.92--dc23
[B]

                                                    2015022688

To Lauren, Mia, and Taylor, my deepest gratitude for providing me the means to sort out your mother/grandmother's life, loves, and absolutely fascinating profession.

Contents

Acknowledgments

How does one acknowledge the kindness and charity of so many individuals who knew Louise Serpa and were willing to share their memories and recollections? Without a doubt, the three people who made this project possible were her immediate family: daughters Lauren Serpa and Mia Larocque, plus Louise's grandson, Taylor Grammar. Without their generous contributions and their vivid memories of their mother and grandmother, this book would not exist. They went beyond the mere interview but were always there to answer my questions as I probed deeper into Louise's life.

Lauren and Mia, of course, have a wealth of knowledge about their mother's professional and personal life, particularly since they had to ride in the backseat of their station wagon from one rodeo event to the other during their childhoods, often being awakened in the middle of the night to get on the road to the next competition. Their unstinting kindness in allowing me complete access to their mother's vast collection of materials—such as her calendars, handwritten travel journals, letters, magazine and newspaper articles that have been written about her through the years, plus her photographs, both professional and personal—brought this project to its ultimate conclusion. Thank you for allowing me into your mother's life.

Louise's half sisters, Anne Brown and Wendy Donoghue, also gave me insight into their big sister's time back east in New York and New Jersey.

Tucson Rodeo manager Gary Williams time and again answered my questions about rodeo in general and my numerous inquiries about Louise and her association with La Fiesta de los Vaqueros.

What would I have done without fashion photographer Bruce Weber's knowledge of Louise's expertise with a camera? He thought of her as more than a professional colleague; he considered her his "big sister."

Artist Barbara Rogers, professor emeritus of painting and drawing at the University of Arizona School of Art, also understood Louise's knack with a camera and gave me much-needed background on content and composition.

With my limited knowledge of cameras, I called on my photographer daughter Sue Cleere to teach me the intricacies of Nikon cameras, exposure, motor drives, film sizing, and a lot of other camera nomenclature that left me feeling more than a little ignorant.

Beatrice "Bea" Mason, owner of Lewis Framing Studio in Tucson, became a fast friend of Louise's and was even allowed to frame some of her photographs, although she readily admitted Louise was a very demanding customer.

Author Betty Barr provided me with copies of articles she and Louise had jointly written and photographed detailing Arizona ranch life. She also gave me intimate, often amusing details of their travels together from one ranch site to another. In addition, Betty generously edited a first draft of the manuscript.

I met with rodeo clown Chuck Henson and his wife, Nancy, who gave up their Fourth of July celebration to talk with me at a tiny Mexican restaurant in Oro Valley, Arizona, the only place we could find open on the holiday.

Charlotte Bell, owner of Graham Bell Gallery in Tubac, Arizona, spoke to me at length about her long association with Louise and the numerous showings of Louise's work at Charlotte's shop.

Jack and Aline Goodman invited me into their home and regaled me with stories about the many years Louise's friends all partied together in each other's homes. Other longtime good friends such as Marty Lynch and Eleanor Smith, along with childhood friend Mary Wheelwright, provided much-needed background on Louise's life both before and after she moved to Tucson.

Brenda Griffin's association with Louise was short, but she felt the older woman had practically adopted her. She was a frequent guest in Louise's home and readily shared memories of their time together.

My thanks to Melissa Harris, Louise's editor at Aperture Foundation Publishers, for allowing me to use many of Louise's quotes from the book *Rodeo*. Throughout this manuscript, quotations of Louise's not otherwise noted are from the text of *Rodeo*.

To all the newspaper and magazine writers who found Louise a fascinating subject and continually wrote about her career and her lifestyle, I thank you for bringing this wonderful woman into the limelight so that others could appreciate her strength and endurance.

Many people had their hands on this book before it was published. To my editors, Erin Turner and Lynn Zelem, I appreciate your kindness, expertise, and attention to detail. Readers such as Betty Barr, Barbara Marriott, and my dear husband, Bob, found discrepancies that I missed even though I must have read the manuscript at least a dozen times.

Other people who contributed to this book with their memories of Louise prefer to remain in the background. I appreciate all of them for sharing their reminiscences and recollections along with their laughter and their tears as they related story after story of Louise's influence on their lives.

To my husband, Bob, thank you for supporting me in my literary endeavors, tolerating dinnerless evenings, and reading every word I write.

Introduction

Snow fell in large, feathery flakes on Valentine's Day 2012 as I made my way across Tucson to meet Mia Larocque and Lauren Serpa, Louise Serpa's daughters. Snow is always a phenomenon in the Old Pueblo, but this particular February 14th also happened to be the celebration of Arizona's one hundredth anniversary of attaining statehood. As I made my way around the Catalina Mountains and into the foothills, I could not help but wonder if Louise's children would be receptive to having a book written about their mom so soon after her death. The little I knew about Louise at the time had led me to boldly write to them and ask for a meeting. Since I had written about many of the early women of Arizona and knew the incredible achievements they had made under sometimes extraordinary circumstances, I strongly felt that Louise's story had to be included with their histories as well as in the history of the state.

Louise Larocque Serpa often said she was born "in the wrong place, to the wrong woman, at the wrong time." Ironically she was born the same year, 1925, as the first rodeo held in Tucson. She grew up in New York society with a mother who was never satisfied with her rather lanky, unpolished daughter. As a teenager Louise found contentment and happiness on a Wyoming dude ranch scrubbing toilets, waiting tables, and wrangling cattle, all while falling in love with a handsome cowboy whose first passion was rodeo. Distance and World War II interfered with this budding romance, but not before a series of letters traversed the continent, expressing the undying devotion of these two besotted lovers.

Eighty of these love letters still exist, all written by the cowboy except for one from Louise when she made the final break with the love of her life.

After one summer out west, Louise returned to New York, obtained a degree in music from prestigious Vassar College (she had a wonderful singing voice), married a Yale man—much to her mother's delight—and relinquished all hope of reuniting with the young cowboy and his life on the rodeo circuit. Their love affair, however, continued for many years through several marriages and divorces.

When her first marriage faltered, Louise headed west again. She met another cowboy, married him, and settled on a sheep ranch in Ashland, Oregon. She bore two children before learning of her husband's infidelity.

Moving to Tucson, Arizona, with her daughters, Louise was introduced to photographing rodeos when a friend invited her to watch his children participate in a junior rodeo competition.

She started photographing youngsters as they bounced and bucked on small sheep and calves, then selling the pictures to proud parents, beginning a career that would span fifty years and take her to the highest pinnacles of rodeo photography.

In 1963 she earned her Rodeo Cowboys Association (RCA) card, the first woman sanctioned to shoot inside the arena fencing.

Over the years, she travelled around the Southwest, especially to almost every rodeo in Arizona, photographing four generations of rodeo families. Cowboys looked for her tall, attractive presence in the arena as they climbed aboard a bucking bronc or bull, expecting her to take the best possible shot of their performance.

She expanded her expertise to photographing cutting shows and polo matches, and eventually found herself shooting England's prestigious Grand National Horse Race and the Dublin Horse Show, the first woman allowed to take pictures inside the grounds of these centuries-old events. She also photographed the Sydney Royal Easter Show, a celebration of Australian culture, and again is believed to be the first woman to do so.

In 1982 fashion photographer Bruce Weber saw some of Louise's rodeo photographs while shooting an advertising spread in Tucson. He was so taken with the vividness and stark reality of her pictures that he insisted she come to New York for a gallery showing of her work. Louise credited Bruce with expanding her career beyond dusty western rodeo towns. He arranged an exhibition for her in New York City, spread her name throughout the photography community, and even used her as a model when, as Louise said, "he needed old age and wrinkles." When asked if he had ever mentored his protégé, Bruce scoffed, "I don't know if anyone has ever mentored Louise."

Even today, Bruce finds it difficult to talk about his old friend. When I interviewed him he asked if I had ever met Louise, and when I told him no but that I had come to know and admire her while researching her life, he said it was probably good I did not know her, as he was unsure I could write the book if I knew her too well—I would have liked her too much to be objective.

Yet as I delved deeper into her background and talked to dozens of people who knew her throughout her lifetime, I began to feel Louise's presence in the room and I was delighted to finally meet her.

Louise maintained yearly calendars from 1965 until 2011 detailing her rodeo appearances as well as hair and nail appointments, school activities for her children, social occasions, and doctor visits. Reading through her calendars was like seeing her daily life unfold with each passing year.

In 1994 Aperture Foundation Publishers produced an impressive book of Louise's photographs entitled *Rodeo*. She went to Africa and Australia to shoot wild animals with her camera and travelled to China and Morocco, photographing the history and people of those regions.

In 1999 Louise was inducted into the National Cowgirl Hall of Fame, and in 2002 she received the Tad Lucas Award from the National Cowboy & Western Heritage Museum, presented to women who have done outstanding work in the sport of rodeo. She was compared to world-famous photographer Annie Leibovitz in a 2007 article in *Arizona Highways* magazine: "In the same ways that Annie Leibovitz is the high priestess of celebrity photography, Louise Serpa is the grande dame of rodeo photography."

Her daughter Mia, who has followed her mother into the rodeo arena, camera in hand, knows firsthand, "There's no better way to experience the action and emotion of rodeo than through the eyes of Louise Serpa."

Louise was interviewed numerous times in newspapers and magazines and had several documentaries produced about her eclectic life and love of rodeo. She was not shy about expressing herself. Because she had so much to say during her lifetime, I considered her words carefully as I progressed with my research. Eventually I realized that this book was turning into a pleasant, albeit rather lengthy, conversation with Louise. I have used her very words when possible and wherever applicable. With permission from Aperture, many of the quotes are from her book *Rodeo*.

In 2009 Louise was diagnosed with cancer, but even as she underwent chemotherapy treatments, lost her hair, and walked with a cane, she never stopped snapping pictures. She continued to photograph the Tucson Rodeo through 2011, when she finally let go of her camera and hung up her hat.

She opened doors for women in photography as well as in rodeo. Her legacy hangs in galleries around the country. Her legions of admirers, including the rodeo riders she captured with her ever-present camera, will not let her be forgotten.

Louise at the Tucson Rodeo circa 1998
COURTESY OF SHARI VAN ALSBURG

Chapter 1

Never don't pay attention.

"Bulls weigh a ton. I've had one on my chest, so I know. He came out of the chute, took one look at me, and made a beeline my way. Thank God he didn't have horns."[1]

The year was 1963 when Louise Serpa stared the powerful and uncontrollable bull in the eye. She was photographing an amateur rodeo in Boulder City, Nevada, shortly after receiving accreditation from the Rodeo Cowboys Association, allowing her to photograph RCA events inside the arena. Up until then she had been relegated to shooting outside the restrictive fencing, limiting the angle of her lens and keeping her several yards from the action. She wanted to get closer to the animals and the riders, down on the ground so she could shoot up as a bucking bronc kicked and reared, trying to displace the cowboy on its back. She wanted to see the sweat on a bull's back and feel its breath on her camera lens. Only then did she feel she had a chance to get a good shot.

She waited until the last possible moment to make her escape. Unfortunately Louise had nowhere to go. As the bull made its charge, she scrambled to climb the arena fence, but it was packed with cowboys—no room for even a slim female body. The sixteen-hundred-pound animal, rider still digging his heels into its beefy, muscular back, snagged her right in the seat of her pants, rudely tossing her about eight feet in the air.

"Oh, is that all there is to it?" she blithely mused as she sailed upward, curling herself around a brand-new Leica camera—the only camera she owned at the time. As she landed with a solid thud on the dirt-packed arena floor, the bull charged, shoving its prey into the ground, stomping her with all its weight. One hoof came down hard on her chest, just below her throat. "Mushed me down pretty much," she remembered, splitting her sternum and breaking several ribs.

Finally several cowboys managed to get the bull away from her, "got me out of the ground and shook me off and set me down again." Right about then the announcer shouted over the loudspeaker, "Did you get his picture, Louise, or should we run him through again?"

She did get the photograph, "one showing the bull was dead earnest and coming right at me. I don't know why he was mad at me. I didn't do anything to him."

Wracked with pain, Louise continued to shoot the rodeo for the rest of the day before heading to the hospital.

"I had no idea how badly I was hurt. I knew it was hard to get my breath—but that was all."

Many a rodeo cowboy has split his sternum by being tossed around and thrown from a bucking horse or bull. The usual treatment is to bind the chest to keep everything intact. This was the first time, however, the doctor had treated a woman for this particular injury, and he had a devil of a time determining how to bandage Louise's chest around her female anatomy.

"I'll never forget that doctor scratching his head trying to figure out how the hell to tape me," she laughed. He finally maneuvered a figure-eight bandage around her body, the best he could do.

The following day, sore and bruised, Louise walked back into the arena to shoot the remainder of the rodeo, determined to finish her job. It had turned cold overnight and every time she shivered in the crisp morning air, excruciating pain shot through her battered body. One of the cowboys noticed her discomfort and produced a flask filled with brandy to brace her coffee so she could make it through the day. She would have preferred tequila, her drink of choice, but the brandy would have to do. It was the coming night, however, that bothered Louise even more.

After the rodeo she had to head back home to Tucson, Arizona, three hundred miles away, where her two young daughters were waiting for her.

The cowboys told her to start for home but if she felt she could not make it, to pull off on the side of the road and leave her lights on. One of them would be by to take her the rest of the way. "And that was rodeo to me," she said. "They would give you all kinds of hell and tease you up a storm. But once they did that, you knew you were accepted and they always checked on you if anything happened."

The incident with the bull took its toll on her for the rest of the year. She was skittish around the animals and found herself retreating to safety before she got the perfect shot. "I'd be gone after one exposure," she said, "up a fence, a telephone pole, a tree—anything I could find to get up, without even knowing how I got there. It took me a long time to get over that. I was being a coward, basically. You know, you can't take very good pictures when you are running.

"I knew if I cried or acted like a woman, I'd never be allowed into the arena again. This was my first trial by fire. And it was good. The one thing I knew I could not do, being the first woman photographer permitted in a rodeo arena, was cry, or act afraid or injured, or anything else. I had to do like the guys did, or I wasn't going to be allowed back in the arena."

Louise in the 1960s with her Nikon
COURTESY OF SERPA FAMILY

Louise learned a valuable lesson from that bull, an experience that stayed with her for the next fifty years. "Never don't pay attention," she often said. "If you get run over as a photographer, that's too bad, that's your own risk you take. You cannot get in the way of the action that's going on. It isn't fair to the cowboys because they've got too much money and pride invested."

By this time in her life, the thirty-seven-year-old had ventured far from her beginnings—born into New York society, matriculating at prestigious Vassar College, marrying a Yale man. How did she end up out west with her nose in the dirt, her boots covered in dust, wearing Levi's and a wide-brimmed western hat encircled with bright silver rondures? It was a life free of societal demands, no mother to tell her she would never amount to anything, answering to no one but herself. Even a charging bull could not dissuade her from the path she had chosen.

[1] The quotes in this chapter are taken from the following sources: *Rodeo* by Louise Serpa, 2007 interview with *Arizona Highways* magazine, and 2004 Rodeo Historical Society interview.

Chapter 2

I was born in the wrong place, to the wrong woman, at the wrong time.

New York City in the 1920s reveled in an era of prosperity. Towering buildings grew overnight against the city skyline as construction struggled to keep up with a growing influx of immigrants from both Europe and the American South. The city was a mecca for manufacturers and merchants.

Prohibition still existed but did not stop bootleggers from exploiting a thriving business in the speakeasies that lined city streets from Manhattan to Brooklyn and the Bronx. It was the heyday of the flapper era, the Jazz Age, and the Harlem Renaissance.

The suffrage movement was at its peak, with women entering the workforce in droves. In 1920 all across the country, women exercised their right to vote for the first time.

Just before Louise's birth in 1925, one of these career-minded women was twenty-one-year-old Louise Yandell Barber, who entered New York City on the arm of her new husband, twenty-four-year-old well-to-do stockbroker Joseph Larocque Jr. Joseph would eventually become part of the Office of Strategic Services, which was established in 1942 and later evolved into the Central Intelligence Agency.

Joseph and Louise Barber Larocque on their wedding day

The couple had married on April 22, 1924, and immediately established a life of affluence and status in the heart of New York society. Louise Larocque had aspirations as an interior designer and learned her craft well. She was brilliant, beautiful, and, according to her relatives, not always the most pleasant person to be around. The only important things in life, according to young Mrs. Larocque, were who you married, his profession, and your social standing.

On December 15, 1925, twenty months after her marriage, Louise gave birth to her first child, a daughter she named after herself.

Little Louise Yandell Larocque struggled for her mother's affection. Criticized, scolded, and told she would never amount to anything, she often rebelled at her mother's displeasure at having to care for a child when she herself was barely an adult. According to young Louise ("Ludie" or "Loudie," as she was called by family and friends), her mother was the "prize snob of the world" and almost impossible to please.

"I was born in the wrong place, to the wrong woman, at the wrong time," she lamented to a reporter from the *Fort Worth Business Press* in 1999. "I always hated the city, hated trying to be something I wasn't."

Even her friends commiserated with Ludie over her mother's dominance, her habit of always telling the child what she could and could not do. One friend recalled the elder Louise Larocque as "very dictatorial" and "sort of famous as being a difficult mother."

Nearly nine years later, when her mother wanted a divorce and headed for Reno, Nevada, the divorce capital of the world at the time, young Ludie went with her.

Divorce was still frowned upon in the 1930s. States such as New York made it an almost impossible procedure, requiring the complaining spouse to provide proof of an adulterous

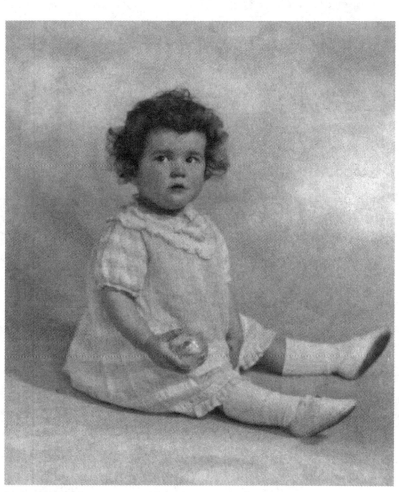

Louise Yandell Larocque around age two
COURTESY OF SERPA FAMILY

affair, and then making him or her endure a yearlong waiting period before the divorce was granted. Nevada, on the other hand, seizing the opportunity to bolster its economy during the dark days of the Great Depression, invited divorce seekers into the state by offering a slew of grounds, including adultery, mental cruelty, insanity, desertion, neglect, impotency, drunkenness, conviction of a felony, and living apart for three years. None of these charges required proof that the accusations were true.

The only requirement Nevada demanded was residency for six weeks. Divorce ranches, later known as dude ranches, sprang up, particularly in the Reno area, comfortable lodgings offering a variety of amenities and a staff willing to cater to wealthy clientele who were waiting out the required number of days to receive a signed Decree of Divorce from the Washoe County Courthouse.

As she later remembered the event in an *Arizona Highways* interview, the then nine-year-old Ludie described the place she and her mother stayed in Virginia City, Nevada, just a few miles down the road from Reno, as a "dusty little dude ranch—but I thought I had died and gone to heaven." For the first time in her young life she was allowed to run at will, get dirty to her heart's content, and ride horses until she became proficient at handling the big steeds. "It was just bliss," she told a *Tucson Citizen* reporter in 2005. "I never had a better time."

The youngster saw her first rodeo in Nevada, and although her love of the sport did not surface at the time, it must have left a deep memory that would emerge a few years down the road.

On July 15, 1935, Louise Larocque obtained her divorce from Joseph. Mother and daughter headed back to the bright lights of New York City.

Ludie's school years began at Miss Chapin's School "for small girl snobs," she delighted in saying. Every summer, her mother sent her off to an all-girls camp to get her out of the way.

Louise, age ten

COURTESY OF SERPA FAMILY

In fact, all of the schools the youngster attended were for girls only, which is why in a 1967 *Arizona Daily Star* interview she mused, "Maybe that helps explain why I ended up in a man's world."

She spent her last high school years in Owings Mills, Maryland, a suburb of Baltimore, attending Garrison Forest School. Founded in 1910, Garrison prides itself on an excellent academic curriculum, plus a highly competitive riding program. But those who knew her at that time do not remember whether Ludie took riding lessons at Garrison. She did sing in the school choir, as she had been born with a deeply romantic and expressive singing voice. And she also was somewhat of a demon on the basketball court.

By this time World War II was raging across Europe. Pearl Harbor had been bombed, sending thousands of US servicemen into the Pacific and European theaters. Businesses floundered as men left in droves to fight for their country. Women took over factory jobs to keep industries in production, drove buses and cabs, and ran family businesses.

Graduating from Garrison in the spring of 1943, Ludie joined a handful of her classmates who had been invited to spend the summer on the Wyoming ranch of one of her schoolmate's relatives. The rancher was struggling to run his spread after most of his cowhands had joined the war effort, so this was not to be a relaxing vacation but a working summer. With her mother surprisingly agreeing to the idea, seventeen-year-old Ludie headed off to the dude ranch in Cody, Wyoming, a town founded in 1895 by the famous William "Buffalo Bill" Cody, Civil War soldier, Indian scout, buffalo hunter, and creator of *Buffalo Bill's Wild West* show.

Through his friendship with President Theodore Roosevelt, Bill Cody bolstered the economy of the town, situated about fifty miles from Yellowstone National Park, by encouraging the establishment of the Bureau of Reclamation and the building of the Shoshone Dam and Reservoir, which was later renamed the Buffalo Bill Dam and Reservoir. In this environment, this giddy handful of wealthy, well-cared-for young women washed dishes, waited tables, and cleaned bathrooms on the sprawling Valley Ranch that lay on the south fork of the Shoshone River. They also learned how to wrangle cattle and helped entertain easterners who came west to enjoy the wide-open spaces for a short while.

Free of her mother's continuous criticism, Ludie reveled in the unrestricted lifestyle that permeated western culture. "[We] rode every chance we got," she told *Southwest Art* magazine in 2004. "The six weeks on the ranch changed my life."

Before long a young, wiry cowboy full of endearing charm and ruggedness swooped in on the young women. Lex Connelly took one look at tall, leggy Ludie, who nicely filled out a pair of Levi's and loved to ride as much as he did, and quickly staked his claim, sweeping her off her feet and into the arms of love for the first time.

An easterner by birth, James Ale "Lex" Connelly was born March 5, 1926, in Bryn Mawr, Pennsylvania. When he was ten the family headed west. His high school years were spent attending the prestigious New Mexico Military Institute (NMMI) in Roswell, where his expertise with horses made him a natural on the polo grounds. At the beginning of the war he wanted to join the Marine Corps but was told to wait until he was eighteen. The summer of 1943, with one more school year to complete, and with his proficiency as a horseman, Lex landed a job working at Wyoming's Valley Ranch.

Lanky and muscular, with a strikingly good-natured grin, he attracted the attention of all the young girls that summer. But it was the equally athletic Ludie who caught Lex's eye; the two were drawn to each other from the moment they met.

Lex's first love, however, was rodeo. "When he told me he was going into rodeo," Louise said, "I thought, *What nonsense, what a waste of time.*" As their romance flourished with teenage innocence (she told one of her friends he was a great kisser), she encouraged Lex to finish college and become a writer, apparently something he was very good at and aspired to achieve. "Forget about the rodeo," she admonished.

At the end of the summer Lex returned to New Mexico, completed his education, and signed on with the US Marines. Ludie rejoined her quarrelsome mother in New York before heading to Vassar College.

Initially, the two young lovers wrote each other almost daily, professing their love and planning a future together. Few of Ludie's letters to Lex survive today, as he was forced to lighten his load after enlisting in the Marine Corps and boarding the battleship *Alabama* headed for the Pacific. But Ludie treasured every letter Lex wrote to her. It is a fatalistic love story, never quite resolved but ending in heartbreak and tragedy.

Chapter 3

If our being together is meant to be, then I believe the time will come.

Once Ludie and Lex left Wyoming, letters and a few telephone calls were their only connections with each other. They made several attempts to meet, either in New Mexico, where Lex's mother lived, or for Lex to come to New York. But the war made travel problematic, sometimes almost impossible.

As Ludie set off for Vassar and Lex continued his studies at NMMI, their actions and undertakings took them in different directions, and the letters that still exist today reflect the distance that began to separate them, both physically and emotionally. The innocence of the letters reflects the war years in which two teenagers tried, desperately and vainly, to strengthen a long-distance relationship.

"You've been gone almost thirty-six hours now, darling," Lex wrote shortly after Ludie left Wyoming. "I've tried to keep myself really busy so that I couldn't think too much about you."

In this same letter he talks about her insistence that he give up drinking. "I'm sure glad you made that no drinking pledge. I've known I'd better quit for quite a while, but this is what I needed to give me the strength to go [sic] it, which I've never had before."

In a later letter as he was on his way to Pueblo, Colorado, to attend a rodeo, he reassured Ludie he continued to honor his vow of abstinence. "I'm still on the wagon, but I heard faint rumors that you girls downed one rum-cake after the other en route" (probably on their way home from Wyoming on the train).

In another letter Lex reassured Ludie that he still loved her. "Darling, as I've said before, only time will tell if our love is strong enough to survive the darkness. We can't truthfully say anything else. But, I can say that I've never looked forward to or wanted anything quite so much."

As for being the wife of a rodeo cowboy, Ludie apparently determined she would be more than content to share this type of existence with Lex. "I'm glad you think you could be happy in my life, if you really do, for I can think of nothing better than teaching you it," he wrote to her. "There is really nothing spectacular about it . . . We get up, eat breakfast, go to the grounds, come back after the afternoon show, take a bath, eat dinner, go to the night show, come back, have a milk shake at the corner drug store, and go to bed.

"I love and miss you more than I can express with pen and ink."

Ludie must have asked him what he wanted for Christmas that year, for he responded, "It's easy to answer your question about what I want for Xmas. I want you, Ma." He often addressed her as "Ma" or "Trudie Shane," although the reference of the latter is unknown. "Next to that I want a real good picture of you close up. . . . Tomorrow, I'll try to get a ring for you, but the supply is a bit scant." Louise recorded several songs that she apparently had sent to Lex, for he added, "One of your records is playing now. I bet they're played 20 times a day.

"Full well do I realize, darling, that we may not see each other till after the war," Lex wrote. "You don't have to worry

Lex Connelly
COURTESY OF SERPA FAMILY

about me forgetting you or anything about you. Never, even if I tried, could I forget this past summer nor the happiness you brought me in it. As I've said before, only time will show the final results of our love. There are too many limiting features to know now—but I do know what I think, and that I'm surer of this than I've ever been of anything of the kind—much surer. This I say frankly, perhaps even brutally so, but maybe it'll help to ease the question you had in your mind."

The couple talked about Lex coming east to enlist in the Marine Corps, but Lex felt there was little chance he would make it. "I'll try everything I can to get back there," he wrote, "but you better not get any hopes up. I know that means maybe—even probably—not seeing you till things are over."

Lex looked for any opportunity to ride in a rodeo, even if it meant fleeing the school grounds. "Sunday there was a jackpot and matched roping about 65 miles from Roswell. I told a few lies and got off for the day and we went. The jackpot was wide open, 16 won it, and most of the good boys went out. I had a chance to win, but my calf fell down and my horse ran over it and that was that."

That first November apart Ludie apparently wrote she wanted to come west for the holidays, but Lex felt it unwise. This was her debutante year, and he was astute enough to realize that if he encouraged her not to attend these events, he would never stand a chance of winning over her parents.

"In your letters you've been talking about coming out here at Xmas," he wrote.

There is nothing Mom would like better, so quell your fears there, and I needn't express my own obvious feelings on the matter, but Loudie you'd better forget it. If it was some other Xmas it might be very different but this is your coming-out year. Such things may be considered silly by some, but nevertheless they are existant [sic] customs that are strongly alive. For seventeen years your mother, your father, the rest of the family and, for almost as long, I'll wager, you yourself have waited for and planned for this time. It all means far too much to them, and to you, wether [sic] you realize it or not, for you just to pull out. You've lived your life "society" and, like it or not, will be for an indefinite time to come. Don't you see, Trudie Shane, you can't just shirk it by missing your coming out?

She did not go west that winter. According to one newspaper article, she was introduced to society at New York's Junior Assembly in 1943.

In January 1944 Lex graduated from NMMI, and he enlisted in the Marine Corps that March. "The Marines will call me sometime between April 1st and 20th," he wrote, "and in the interim we're going to El Paso, the end of this month [for a rodeo] and, Marine Corps willing, Phoenix [to another rodeo] which starts April 13th, and we'll take our own horses for a pleasant change."

The love-struck couple planned to meet in Wyoming in the summer of 1944 after Lex got out of boot camp, but he did not get the expected furlough. By September he was in Hawaii preparing to ship out on the battleship *Alabama*. Joining the Marine Corps seemed to mature Lex, and his letters began to reflect a more thoughtful and serious young man. (Lex spent his first three months on board the USS *Alabama* in the Pacific, on the Ulithi Atoll in the Western Caroline Islands, supporting the infantry off the shores of Okinawa, and bombing Minami Daito Jima, about two hundred miles east of Okinawa.)

Now, I shall be very frank with you, and tell you the truth—that it will be two years before I even have the chance to see you, for it will be that long almost surely before I get back to the States. A lot of boys stay longer than that. Now, that is a long time, a very long one. . . . These next two years are probably the best two of our young lives. The Marine Corps has decided what I shall do with mine, but you are more or less free to determine how yours will be spent, and I should like to help your decision, at least express my views.

I would like you to live these years a little differently than the past one, in which we kept thinking we'd see one another before too long. I want to ask you to, in a sense, put me out of your mind. Not, as I had thought about saying, as if you had never met me. Definitely not that, but more as if I had just passed from the world somehow, which, as far as seeing you is concerned, I have. Live these two years more or less as if you never would see me again. Then when I come back, which, of course I shall, for there is little danger where I'm bound, I will never have the feeling that I have made you waste the best years you have, and yet nothing between us will be harmed any more than if you sat in your room gazing at my repulsive face and knitting socks.

Lex's December 1944 letter reinforced his insistence that they realize their short summer romance was not sufficient enough on which to build a lifetime.

Then, who do you think you love, the guy you knew for six weeks, or the one you've admittedly "built up" for seventeen months? After all, you hardly had a fair chance to learn any of my many bad points.

You say you are prepared to live out West, and know what that means. There won't be any of your friends there . . . and very few of your kind. A girl such as you never quite forgets her background, and always misses it a little. It was smart of you to try and get into rodeoing as much as possible. I congratulate you again. Now you know you'd never like it, and yet that's probably what I'll be doing if I can get good enough to make a go of it. It may be a sorry way of life, but it's better than wrangling dudes or gambling.

Things look very much against a future for us together.

This is, I fear, a most dismal letter. However, you asked for the straight dope, and here it is—three pages of it. Honestly, I don't know if I love you or not, or even if I know what love is. I'm probably a damn fool if I don't, but I can't honestly say I'm sure I do. However, I do know that things are very much against you ever being happy with me. Of course, as you say, we'll have to wait to make anything final until we see each other. Meanwhile, wouldn't it be better for you to assume that we're not in love than that we are in love?

P.S. Your fruitcake arrived—the best I've ever tasted. The Marine Division enjoyed it no end, and I heartily thank you on behalf of us all.

The one letter known to exist from Ludie to Lex is dated January 1, 1946. Apparently they were planning on meeting in New York, but she advised him not to come. Twenty-one-year-old Ludie finally admitted it was time to end the relationship.

The summer we had together was the happiest one of my life ever, so happy and complete with you, that it doesn't seem possible that it was real. There has been no one else but you since and there is no one else now darling. I want you to believe these things. What you gave me in spirit and love, I can never forget, nor can I forget how much I loved you, more than anything or anyone in the world. It is strange that these very facts make me say "don't come" now . . . and yet is it so strange? If you come and we discovered that we were in love, what then? From a purely realistic standpoint, we couldn't get married for quite a few years more. I know that neither you nor I can be idealistic about marriage—we have seen too much unhappiness in our own families, and know what mis-takes can mean.

I have fought with myself for a while now—wanting you to come yet knowing it would be best if you didn't. It seems cowardly to take this stand at such a late date and it's hard because I don't know how you feel about coming.

Oh Lex there is so much I want to say and can't. I could ask you to consider that I'm wrong, but I won't because I've got to use my head. Whether this is to be the absolute end or not I'll leave up to you. Perhaps it would be best to quit now when we can both remember what we had as we want to remember it. I am a fatalist and you said once you were too. If our being together is meant to be, then I believe the time will come. If not, I have no reason to regret a minute of the past two and a half years.

Darling, darling please tell me I'm right in this. It's so late and I'm sorry to have messed everything up. I want so to be right, to be wise and calm about it. I hate all this indecision, fear and tenseness. It may be hard to believe but I like to laugh and be gay more than the average guy. I'm not always as serious-minded as I have appeared to be in the past. Chalk it up to an attempt to rectify any mistakes I have made and any unhappiness I may have caused you. I wouldn't blame you for being mad as hell at me now and if you want to swear at me—swear away mi lad. I'm stout, I can take it and am up for more. For Pete's sake let me know how you feel.

Until then as ever, Loudie

This was certainly not the end of their love affair, as Lex and Louise continued to stay in touch through the years, although there are only a handful of additional letters in which they continued to express their love. The match that was supposedly made in heaven, however, never materialized as the two went their separate ways, reuniting whenever they had a chance. Years later, Louise acknowledged it was the brash, sexy, teenage Lex Connelly who first instilled in her a love of rodeo that remained with her the rest of her life.

Chapter 4

Rodeo stayed with me from then on.

Although Ludie entered Vassar College in the fall of 1943, shortly after returning from Wyoming, her desire was to attend the Juilliard School of Music, as she felt she was not truly whole unless she was singing. Her melodic voice had already stirred interest among school administrators, who encouraged her to pursue a musical career.

Her mother, however, vetoed the idea of Juilliard, insisting that prestigious Vassar was where all high-society girls matriculated. Consequently the youngster left her mother's New York City home on East Seventy-Second Street and enrolled in the upstate college.

Vassar sits on one thousand acres in Poughkeepsie, about seventy-five miles north of New York City. It is consistently ranked among the top liberal arts colleges and acknowledged as one of the most beautiful schools in the country. Founded in 1861, it became the pioneering standard for women's higher education.

During World War II Vassar offered its students the opportunity to complete their bachelor degrees in three years instead of four, which meant attending classes in forty-week sessions each academic year. The graduates were then expected to go out and "make a difference in our world." Ludie and her friends accepted the challenge.

"It was tough during the war," remembers Mary Wheelwright, a longtime friend of Ludie's who also recalls very little vacation time during those three academic years. She and Ludie, along with six other girls, roomed together in Vassar's Cushing Hall, named after librarian Florence Cushing, valedictorian of the 1874 class and Vassar's first graduate to serve on the school's board of trustees.

Mary and Ludie were part of the Daisy Chain, freshman girls selected by the senior class as the most attractive incoming students.

Ludie matriculated in music at Vassar and recorded several songs during this time. Apparently these were the records she sent to Lex that he mentioned listening to in his dorm room in New Mexico. Today the few original recordings that still exist are a little scratchy and somewhat warped, yet her voice comes through strong and sure in songs such as "Summertime," "My Hero," "I Don't Know Why," "I'm Gonna Let You Go," "Teasin'," "I'm Old Enough for a Little Lovin'," "Heart of My Heart," and "Night & Day."

She minored in art at Vassar, but even Ludie admitted she could do little more than copy a picture of a piece of fruit, that she had no talent for developing ideas of her own. She did confess, however, to becoming rather proficient at clay sculpting.

She missed Lex terribly during her time at Vassar and resolved to learn more about rodeos so when they did meet again, she would better understand why he loved the sport so much. Since Vassar touted its students as a "breed apart" for their independence of thought and inclination to "go to the source" in search of answers, she did just that by sneaking out of school to attend rodeos at New York's Madison Square Garden.

Lex, of course, was overseas, but many of his friends worked the rodeo circuit that came into Madison Square Garden for three weeks each fall. On those crisp autumn evenings when the rodeo was in town, Ludie broke out of Cushing Hall and hopped the train in Poughkeepsie for New York City. From the station she walked the short distance to Madison Square Garden, often meeting up with friends such as a classmate from Garrison Forest School whose boyfriend participated in the rodeo.

"I loved a lot of the people who were involved in the rodeo," she told *Vassar Quarterly* in a 1995 interview. "They were the free spirits that I supposed I always wanted to be. They lived the life they loved. . . . Rodeo stayed with me from then on."

Ironically, one of the performers Ludie saw at the Garden was bronc and trick rider Tad Lucas, whose recognition as "Rodeo's First Lady" already had made her a legend by the time Ludie saw her perform in 1945. Lucas's fame would play an important role later in Ludie's life.

After a performance Ludie would ride back to Poughkeepsie, dutifully finishing her homework on the train before arriving back at school around two in the morning. The school's night watchman at the time happened to be from Wyoming and an avid rodeo fan. As long as she gave him the results of the rodeo and showed him the day sheets, he let her into the dorm and said nothing about her nightly excursions.

During Christmas break from school in 1943, after Lex had told her not to come west for the holidays and perhaps feeling disappointed and more than a little sad, Ludie defiantly donned a tight-fitting, bright red dress and made her way into New York City to meet friends at a nightclub. Wanting to show off some of the newly acquired western skills she had learned in Cody, the very attractive and shapely Ludie boldly stepped up to the bar and planted her foot firmly on the foot rail. Out of her tiny purse she pulled a match to light her cigarette. Confidently and shamelessly, she struck the match on her rear end, a trick she had learned from the cowboys on the dude ranch. In an instant the match caught fire and so did her red dress, scorching the fabric across her backside. "I could never be what I was supposed to be," was her only lament. "I was not New York society."

Her singing talent allowed her to explore music, from opera to jazz to popular show tunes. During the school year she spent endless hours in the Skinner Hall of Music at Vassar and sang whenever she got the opportunity, often boasting she vocalized "for cigarettes in every bar from Arlington [New York] to Poughkeepsie." Her desire at the time was a career singing on the radio or on stage.

She told *Tucson Lifestyle* magazine in a 2005 interview, "My mother disapproved violently of my singing in public. A lady did not sing on the stage, which is really what I wanted to do. Musical comedy at that point was pretty big stuff."

The war provided Ludie with opportunities to sing with the United Services Organization (USO), which has given GIs a "home away from home" since 1941. Entertaining the troops became another way to support the war effort; camp shows became popular both at home and overseas. She tried to join the Women's Auxiliary Ferrying Squadron (WAFS), which was formed in 1942, even taking flying lessons and earning her solo wings, but since the young schoolgirl was not yet twenty-one, the WAFS turned her down. In 1943 the WAFS was integrated into the Women Airforce Service Pilots (WASP). This group was disbanded in 1944.

Consequently Ludie sang in USO service clubs along the East Coast from Baltimore to New York. In 2004, she told the Rodeo Historical Society, "If the Marines were in town you sang one type of song, or if Australians were in town, boy you were in for a wonderful night."

One evening after singing at an officers' club in New York City, she said she was just about to board the bus to take her home when "this hairy arm reached in and pulled me backwards off the bus." The sergeant politely apologized. "I'm sorry to do this to you, Ms. Larocque, but my captain would like to talk to you."

Before she knew it she was seated before a good-looking, huge man who was introduced to her as Captain Hank Greenberg. They had a drink and exchanged polite conversation until Ludie said she had to go home. She was late for supper that evening, and her stepfather (her mother had remarried) asked why. When she told him she had been asked to have cocktails with Hank Greenberg, her stepfather almost knocked over his own drink and eagerly asked when she was bringing him home for dinner. That was her first indication she had just met Detroit Tigers power hitter "Hammerin'" Hank Greenberg, one of the most dominant baseball hitters of the day.

Greenberg had been drafted in 1940, baseball's first American League player to be drafted. Honorably discharged in 1941, he reenlisted in the US Air Force two days after Japan bombed Pearl Harbor and served until 1945, the longest duration of any major league player. Unfortunately, he and the attractive young singer shared nothing more than a drink on that lovely evening in New York City.

By the time Ludie returned to Vassar in the fall of 1944, young women across the country were abandoning their tight-fitting girdles, black-and-white saddle oxfords, and immaculate Brooks Brothers sweaters for the more casual clothing of their male counterparts. Men's shirts with their long tails hanging out over snug blue jeans and soft, comfortable moccasins started appearing across the all-girl campus. Ludie was delighted to add Levi's to her eastern wardrobe.

Graduation from Vassar
COURTESY OF SERPA FAMILY

On June 30, 1946, Ludie stood with 353 other graduates as Vassar president Henry Noble MacCracken conferred bachelor degrees on the class of 1946, the largest graduating class to date.

Her mother probably insisted she attend the graduation ball at New York's Waldorf-Astoria Hotel that year. The original establishments, the Waldorf Hotel and the Astoria Hotel, had opened in 1893 and 1897, respectively. The Waldorf-Astoria Ludie walked into that summer evening, however, was inaugurated in 1931 as the world's largest and tallest hotel, a virtual "city within a city." Forty-seven floors high with over fifteen hundred rooms, it was the first hotel to offer room service, influencing the hotel industry around the world.

Ludie had hoped to avoid this ritual, as she had no interest in these social events and doubtless dreaded the long evening that lay before her. Nevertheless, she dutifully slipped on a long flowing gown, high-heeled shoes, and the prerequisite elbow-length gloves and made her way to the ballroom.

As she stood at the top of the long winding staircase and scanned the crowd below, a hint of rebellion played across her face. Since she would be twenty-one years old in December, she had determined it was time to wield her independence. Without thinking twice she hitched up her gown, grabbed the bannister, blithely climbed aboard, and slid sidesaddle down the length of the railing. If she had thought to bring a cowboy hat, she most certainly would have waved it and let out a whoop while sailing down the staircase.

By the time her wild ride ended, Ludie's beautiful white gown was split all the way up the back. Louise Yandell Larocque had decidedly, and defiantly, declared her freedom from New York society.

Chapter 5

We would do almost anything for money at the time.

"If I couldn't sing, I didn't want to do much," Louise said of her life after the war. In November 1946 she worked for a short while as a counter sales clerk (now known as a ticket agent) for KLM Royal Dutch Airlines, earning $40 a week. In March of the following year, she represented KLM at air shows in Detroit and Chicago and was still working for the airline that November, now earning a grand total of $50 a week. But she was also making the rounds of New York nightclubs, as well as singing for organizations and at churches any chance she could, much to her mother's chagrin. This was not what a New York society girl did with her life.

She may have sung at Sammy's, a boozy haven in the heart of the Bowery, also known as the poor man's Stork Club. According to a 1944 *Life* magazine article, Sammy's was home to the city's derelicts, drunks, and downtrodden, all warmly welcomed by owner Sammy Fuch, who had opened his establishment in 1934 and became the patron saint of local bums. The bar, which sat between Houston and Stanton Streets, also fascinated the uptown crowd, who came to watch those less fortunate stagger in and out of the drinking establishment at all hours of the day and night. Some who knew Louise around this time believe she did sing there occasionally, although there is also a faction that believes she sang at the more tony Stork Club, owned by Sherman Billingsley in the heart of New York City. Photographs exist of her patronizing both establishments.

Lex Connelly, now out of the Marine Corps, eventually showed up in town, rekindling intimate feelings that had caught fire between the two young lovers back in Wyoming. But Lex was now married and Louise, respecting his marriage vows, had no intention of destroying the union. Distraught, she knew she "had to put him out of my mind."

Through the years, the two continually remained out of sync in their relationship. But they "kept up always," Louise said in her Rodeo Historical Society interview. "He always knew where I was and I always knew where he was."

Louise's mother had married Gilbert Goodwin Browne, a banker, and produced two more daughters, Wendy and Anne. Louise absolutely adored her stepfather, affectionately calling him "Pappy." But this put another dagger between her and her mother, as the elder Louise was openly jealous of the relationship.

Over twenty years younger than their half sister, Wendy and Anne Browne admired Louise, although both women later admitted that the age gap prevented a close sisterly bond.

"One of the things that my sister gave to me and to my world view was that there was a sense of a different place and a different way to life than living in New York City," Anne recalls. "Her presence in my life, occasional through it was, provided me with a sense of a future that I could actually live with."

Floundering after learning of Lex's marriage, and to ease tension between her and her mother, Louise dutifully married

Louise and Phil DuVal
COURTESY OF SERPA FAMILY

Philip DuVal in April 1948, "a very nice, unsuspecting man from Yale."

The elaborate wedding took place at New York City's St. James Episcopal Church. Wearing a flowing satin gown with a lace mantilla and looking all the world like a devout and soon-to-be devoted wife, Louise demurely walked down the aisle. Four-year-old Wendy served as flower girl in a bright pink taffeta dress that matched the calamine lotion covering her chicken pox. Anne was just a baby.

The newlyweds settled in New Canaan, Connecticut, one of the wealthiest communities in the country.

For four years Louise tried to be happy, but knew she had done her husband "a terrible disservice." The marriage was not a good fit for either of them. Finally, in 1952, she left Philip and headed for Nevada to obtain a divorce, just as her mother had done seventeen years prior.

Although they found it impossible to live together, Louise and Philip remained friends the rest of their lives. Every year on the anniversary of their wedding, Philip, who eventually remarried, sent Louise flowers.

Louise in Scottsdale

"I came out to live in Nevada in '52," Louise told reporter Betty Barr in a 2000 interview, "and there was a team roping going on in the valley every weekend and I had a little tinker toy camera. It was a $27 Argus fixed lens." The camera is now in the National Cowgirl Hall of Fame Museum.

Back in 1988 she wrote an article about her beginnings in Nevada for her alma mater *Chapin School Bulletin*. "There was jack pot roping every week down the road . . . The cowpokes would want to see how their horses were setting up so I would go take pictures of them. I knew the timing and what they were supposed to be doing, even if my photography wasn't techni-cally good."

Cowboys bought her rolls of film, she said, and plied her with beer so she would take pictures of them, allowing them to critique their actions in the ring.

After her divorce was final, Louise returned to New York to pick up her belongings and break her final ties with the city. In the 1988 article she recalled leaving town:

In a six-cylinder Dodge with hope, my hundred-pound hound "Pericles," and a few possessions, I drove into the sunset. The stuff dreams are made of? Well . . . yes, because I was going where I wanted, to live the way I wanted, beholden to no one; an enviable position. Through all the years that followed, no matter how tough the circumstances, I never lost the feeling of being on perpetual holiday nor the joy of living in big free space.

I drove straight to Scottsdale [Arizona]. I had no job, no money to speak of. . . . I found a place to live with three acres of pasture for my horse and it was $75 a month. I worked for a gal who had a wonderful Mexican shop—Mexican clothes and jewelry.

Although it is unproven, some believe that during this time she may have sung at the historic Pink Pony Steakhouse, a Scottsdale landmark since 1947.

The beautiful, svelte, young brunette had no trouble attracting suitors. Before long she had another charming cowboy dangling from her arm—tall, handsome Gordon Rodney "Tex" Serpa. Tex had many of the qualities Louise admired in Lex Connelly and it did not take long for her to decide he was the cowboy she wanted.

Tex traveled to New York to meet her family wearing his cowboy hat and a pair of denim jeans. Louise's mother cringed with embarrassment as she surveyed his permanently dusty boots and an odd string he wore around his neck called a bolo tie. Nine-year-old Wendy Browne, however, thought the good-looking Tex was so handsome that he was the "cat's pajamas."

Tex Serpa at Flying W, 29 Palms

Louise and Tex at Flying W, 29 Palms
COURTESY OF SERPA FAMILY

Louise and Tex married in April 1953. For a few years they lived in the very small town of 29 Palms, California (now spelled Twentynine Palms), located about twenty miles east of Yucca Valley on State Route 62. Renting a stable from Hollywood song-writer Allie Wrubel, the couple ran a string of horses to entertain visiting easterners. They counted actors James Cagney and Ralph Bellamy as their neighbors on Wrubel's Flying W Ranch.

Wrubel had collaborated with lyricist Ray Gilbert on the 1947 Oscar-winning song "Zip-A-Dee-Doo-Dah" from the film *Song of the South*. He was involved in numerous movies during the 1930s and '40s, including *Make Mine Music*, *Duel in the Sun*, *I Walk Alone*, and *Midnight Lace*. Wrubel also wrote such well-known tunes as "The Lady from 29 Palms" (which was not about Louise), "Gone with the Wind," "Music, Maestro, Please," "The Masquerade Is Over," "Mine Alone," and "How Long Has This Been Going On."

When Wrubel wanted to hear what one of his new songs sounded like, he sent for Louise, who said in her interview with the Rodeo Historical Society that she would "race over to the big house, dropping my shovel of manure or whatever I was doing and sing with him." That was the best part of the day for Louise, literally singing for her supper.

Louise and Tex did "anything to make money," she told the *Vassar Quarterly* reporter in 1995, "from digging graves, $35 a grave, to hauling cement block," constantly struggling to stay afloat. Hay for their forty head of horses cost them dearly and meant a day trip to either the small California town of Banning, over 50 miles away, or to Blythe, which was over 125 miles in the opposite direction.

According to Louise in her Historical Society interview, they usually had to write a "completely worthless check for five tons of hay, race back to Twentynine Palms as fast are our big old secondhand truck would go, sell about four ton of it, enough to cover the check, and go back and do it again the next week."

They eventually relocated to Oregon, accepting an offer to rebuild and run a beat-up old ranch, the Walking S, that Louise's stepfather, Gilbert Browne, bought for them near the small community of Ashland, just fifteen miles north of the California state line.

Early pioneers had valued this lush valley at the base of the Siskiyou Mountains with its rich soil and broad, sweeping range-lands. The town of Ashland had been established on the site of an old Shasta Indian village, situated about halfway between Sacramento, California, and Portland, Oregon. The town also profited by lying just north of Siskiyou Pass, part of the original Oregon/California wagon train route and, later, the busy stage-coach and rail lines that ran between Sacramento and Portland.

In Ashland, Louise and Tex's lives revolved around main-taining the Walking S sheep ranch. "All of a sudden," Louise told a reporter for *The Foothills* magazine in 2006, "I became a sheepherder."

She absolutely loved having a place of her own and land to ride and roam to her heart's content. She bottle-fed lambs from a Coke bottle and roamed the property at night armed with a shotgun to keep coyotes from eating her flock.

"It was hard work and I loved every minute of it," she recalled of herding the stock, plowing the fields, and rebuilding the old ranch house. She had found where she belonged. She was part of the West.

On July 21, 1956, Louise gave birth to her first daughter, Lauren Gilbert Serpa. Two and a half years later, on January 29, 1959, a second child, Maria "Mia" Serpa, was born.

Three months after Mia's birth, Tex headed out along the old Oregon Trail as trail master for the reenactment of a journey so many early pioneers had taken over one hundred years before as they headed west seeking a better life. The "On to Oregon Cavalcade" also celebrated Oregon's centennial.

On April 19, 1959, the reenactment of the countless wagon trains that had traveled from Independence, Missouri, to Independence, Oregon, during the 1800s started out across the plains. During the four-month trek, twenty-five to thirty spirited individuals lived in replicas of original prairie schooners as they made their way through Kansas, Nebraska, Wyoming, and Idaho. They spent 130 days and nights crossing wheat-swept grasslands, fording rivers, and climbing the treacherous and tortuous Rocky Mountains. They subsisted on beans cooked over open fires, washed their clothes and themselves in buckets of river water, and slept out in the open.

Traveling fifteen to twenty miles a day, the entourage passed grave markers left for early pioneers who did not survive those initial dangerous trips. Many of the towns the reenactors entered celebrated their arrival with festive barbeques.

Shoshone Indians, once considered the enemy, entertained them with Native dances. On August 15, 1959, the rather worn-out, tired, and dusty travelers culminated their journey by arriving at a momentous celebration in Independence, Oregon.

Wagon master Tex Serpa's expertise with horses made him responsible for selecting the horses and mules that pulled the wagons. He ensured provisions were plentiful throughout the trek and kept the travelers on the trail. His skill with a twenty-foot bullwhip may have had a hand in keeping the peace, although the participants claimed they had too much fun to create any degree of disorder or mayhem.

Tex, however, needed all his talents to keep everyone away from the dangers of modern transportation that moved swiftly down highways, byways, and railroad tracks that they passed. The rather leisurely march hardly resembled the trials and tribulations encountered by those who first made their way across this strange new land. Still, it was a long road and a few mishaps did occur, including the demise of Louise and Tex's marriage.

Certainly a busy man on the trail, Tex did manage to have some fun—a little too much amusement, according to Louise.

Cowboy Tex had a wandering eye and the couple had seen their share of trouble over the last few years, even separating for a time before their second child was born. Louise did not make the historic Oregon Trail trip with Lex but stayed behind to care for toddler Lauren and baby Mia, meeting up with her husband and the wagon train as it pulled into Independence, Oregon. Only later did she learn that Tex had dallied with some of the ladies he met in towns along the way. Whether that contributed to the miscarriage of her next child, a boy, she never knew.

Chapter 6

I couldn't sing in bars anymore.

Tex's scandalous dalliances on the Oregon Trail reenactment were the talk of Ashland, leaving Louise alone, rejected, and determined to get out of town. She sold the ranch, paid off her debts, and drove down the California coast with her two children in the backseat. Her divorce from Tex was final in December 1959.

She had no idea where she was going or how to support her daughters. Some say she poked her finger on a map and it landed on the small, dusty town of Tucson, Arizona. Others are convinced she was looking for any wide-open spaces that would allow her to live in peaceful solitude. After two failed marriages, and with no viable means of support, Louise heavily felt the weight of her responsibilities.

"Suddenly," she said in her 2007 interview with *Arizona Highways*, "I had to figure out how I was going to make a living with two kids."

Quite possibly, her family helped her financially through this crisis, particularly since her mother took her on her first trip to Europe in 1960 while Lauren and Mia stayed with New York relatives. The promise of Louise's artistic abilities surfaced during this trip as she became intrigued with intricate carvings she discovered on ancient structures. After taking copious pictures she returned to the ship as it headed for Capri, only to have the lens fall out of her camera, destroying all the pictures she had taken. She still had a lot to learn about photography.

Soon after arriving in Tucson, Louise was invited to attend a junior rodeo, a sport that allows youngsters to compete by riding a small calf, sheep, or goat that gently bucks and kicks, trying to dislodge its unwelcome guest. The kids have a great time "mutton bustin'" even as they topple off their steeds and onto the soft dirt that has been carefully groomed to keep them from harm.

Junior rodeos usually consist of three age groups: five to twelve, thirteen to fifteen, and sixteen to eighteen. Most of the children who compete in these events come from second- and third-generation rodeo families.

"I'd never even heard of junior rodeo at that point," Louise told the reporter for the *ProRodeo Sports News* in 1999. "I could not believe nobody was taking pictures of the kids coming out riding calves and roping and doing everything the big guys did. It was mindboggling that there were no photographers."

She saw the potential for making a few dollars by taking pictures of the young cowboys and cowgirls as they galloped out of the shoots on their miniature mounts, bouncing up and down like rubber balls, roping just like their dads and big brothers.

She asked officials if she could enter the ring and shoot photographs of the children. At the time, she was still using the little Argus camera she had purchased in Nevada.

Recalling her first rodeo days for reporters from *Arizona Highways* and the *Vassar Quarterly*, Louise said, "I guess the officials didn't see where I could do too much damage. So I got into the ring and for 75 cents apiece, I sold those pictures [5x7 prints] to the parents of the children."

Louise, Lauren, and Mia in Tucson, circa 1962

COURTESY OF SERPA FAMILY

Initially, Louise looked at her new pursuit as a casual hobby, earning a little money but not enough to support her family. Circumstances were looming, however, that turned her diversion into a full-time, demanding, and dangerous profession.

"One night I put Mia to bed after running around the house like crazy," she told the Rodeo Historical Society, "and all of a sudden she started screaming in the middle of the night. That's how fast it took over. She couldn't walk."

Fourteen-month-old Mia had developed juvenile rheumatoid arthritis, also known as juvenile idiopathic arthritis, one of the most common types of arthritis in young children. In this autoimmune disorder that can cause joint pain, swelling, and stiffness, symptoms can last just a few months, or for years. About one in every one thousand children is affected by arthritis each year.

Doctor bills took a toll on Louise's sparse income, and she knew she had to find good work that would pay her escalating expenses. "I had to make money, and I couldn't sing in bars anymore."

She told *Tucson Lifestyle* in 2005, "Making the pastime a career happened by accident, in the truest sense of the word. I wrecked my car, and my youngest daughter got rheumatoid arthritis, and all of a sudden, the little bit of money I had salted away was gone. I had to get to work. I couldn't make enough singing, so I did all sorts of things like paint walls and furniture. None of them did really well, so I went full blast on the photography."

Louise continued to shoot junior rodeos but actively sought photography work elsewhere.

"I did the whole quarter horse circuit for a long time," she told reporter Betty Barr. "Anything that involved a horse, I did it."

The first steed bred in the United States to compete, quarter horses develop large muscles, have great speed and a pleasant disposition, and possess superior intelligence. During the 1670s quarter-mile races became a popular sport in the small towns and villages of colonial America.

As pioneers migrated west these animals were naturals at herding cattle, hauling heavy wagons, and plowing the land. Horse racing grew along with the country, with ranchers favoring the quarter horse for both work and recreation, particularly in rodeo competitions such as cattle roping, steer wrestling, and barrel racing.

Quarter horse shows gave Louise another source of income; she particularly enjoyed going to the competitions in Sonoita, Arizona, the town that claims the longest-running quarter horse show in the United States. There, she and longtime quarter horse breeder Rose Fulton would sit in Rose's car, watch the action, and compare notes on the various horses. Rose died in 1968 at the age of eighty-six. Louise missed her terribly.

Louise was asked to step in for a photographer who did not show up to shoot events at the Southern Arizona International Livestock Association and the Pima County Fair. SAILA, as it was known, was founded in 1934 to support the livestock industry in southern Arizona and northern Mexico. Among its programs, the group sponsored 4-H and Future Farmers of America. Tucson's Rillito Park Racetrack and the Pima County Fairgrounds were once owned by SAILA.

The fair included breed shows, hunter jumper divisions, team roping, cutting horse, and cattle competitions. Louise knew nothing about these contests except that the shows paid much more than photographing rodeos. She was determined to learn everything she could about each and every event.

One of the first things she discovered was that cutting is the ultimate a horse can do. Quarter horses are usually bred for this competition since they have the strength and agility to respond quickly, can turn sharply while trying to keep a cow from returning to the herd, and have what cowboys call "natural cow sense."

In the arena the horse and rider separate a cow from the herd and must keep it isolated for two and a half minutes. The cow, of course, wants no part of this practice and continually tries to return to its mates. The cowboy must leave most of the work up to the horse, and a good cutting horse competes with a sound sense of judgment, expediency, and style, thoroughly enjoying the process.

Hunter-jumper contests were also a new concept for Louise. As she aimed her camera, she watched the horse's appearance, its form and skill at jumping fences, along with its ability to run the course at a fast, even pace.

She thought she did some of her best photography at these competitions, but no one wanted to buy her images. Finally a cowboy named Slim Trent ("a tall drink of water," according to Louise) told her to take her pictures when the horse was on its way down, not going up. That small piece of advice gave her images that were much more animated, and certainly helped her develop the keen eye she needed for sharp, salable photographs. She raised her prices to $7 a picture.

After every show Louise gathered up the rolls of film she had taken, returned to Tucson, and deposited her pictures at Caples camera shop for development. At one time Caples was the largest photographic company in the Southwest. She told the Rodeo Historical Society, "One day I had worked two whole days down in Elfrida, which is a tiny town north and west of Douglas. I had slept in the back of the station wagon and endured the heat and all the rest of this terrible stuff I went through, brought my film home, probably four or five films, to Caples. And their machine ate it, shredded the film. I was so mad and so upset that I figured maybe I had better learn how to develop the film."

Louise set up a darkroom in a closet of her home and, with only an instruction booklet from Kodak, taught herself how to develop film. Eventually she bought a complete darkroom from George Rosenberg, then editor of the *Tucson Citizen* newspaper. In a 2004 radio interview she admitted she still had, and used, much of Rosenberg's original equipment.

She continued to shoot junior rodeos, from tiny tots to high school and college competitions. She told the Rodeo Historical Society, "I had the whole winter run in February and March starting in Yuma, then Scottsdale, then Tucson, then Phoenix, then Globe." If she was lucky she would get up to Denver in January to start the run.

"I'd sleep in the back of my station wagon if there were no motels," she told *Arizona Highways* magazine. "I'd shoot a junior rodeo on Saturday, and another on Sunday." She became so involved with the junior rodeo circuit that when the Arizona Junior Rodeo Association (AJRA) was established in the early 1960s, she became a member of the founding board.

"At the time," she said, "the stock was uneven in quality, and the judging had some problems. So a group of parents and other concerned people formed the organization, complete with a rule book, in order to give kids a fair shake."

"The two junior associations, Little Britches and the Arizona Junior Rodeo Association, are wonderful proving grounds."

On trips out of town, Louise shot up to twelve hours a day, then processed the film that evening. "In those days," she recalled in her Rodeo Historical Society interview, "rodeo was so small you knew everybody on the circuit. They were running from one place to another so fast that I would have the proof sheets out overnight. Many times I have taken duct tape or tinfoil and blacked out a bathroom in a motel and then done the proof sheets overnight, so the guys could look at them the next day." The cowboys clamored for her pictures because her shots showed them where they had made a mistake or how they had handled a certain bull or horse.

Not all of her time, however, was spent taking pictures of cowboys and following rodeo circuits. In late 1961 Hollywood director Sam Peckinpah brought a movie company to Tucson to film *The Deadly Companions*, a western picture starring Maureen O'Hara, Brian Keith, Steve Cochran, and Chill Wills. Peckinpah was looking for a handful of extras, and the stately, stunning Louise landed a small role in the movie that was partly filmed at the Rail N Ranch in Catalina, Arizona, just north of Tucson.

The following year, Louise photographed her first Tucson Rodeo.

Chapter 7

The next thing you know you've got some dame out in the middle of the arena.

There were just a handful of good rodeo photographers before Louise Serpa entered the profession. Ralph Doubleday became the first well-known rodeo photographer by capturing the image of a cowboy in midair. He was followed by DeVere Helfrich, often called the Dean of Rodeo Photographers for his innovative methods. Helfrich held the reins for almost twenty years before retiring in 1962. The *ProRodeo Sports News* claimed he was "the world's greatest rodeo photographer." After his death in 1981, the *News* wrote in its 1982 championship edition that Helfrich "will forever be ranked as one of the top rodeo photographers of all time, no matter who comes along with what degree of talent in the future." He was posthumously inducted into the National Cowboy Hall of Fame in 1991.

Helfrich had photographed the Tucson Rodeo for many years, and no one was going to take his place as long as he wanted to shoot. "I wasn't allowed in the arena at all until DeVere retired," Louise told reporter Betty Barr. She learned all she could from the great photographer, and when he did step down, she got her chance—outside the arena.

By now she was getting compliments for her pictures from both the general public and the more critical eyes of cowboys. One rider even told her, "You take pretty good pictures for a girl." She graciously accepted the compliment.

At the time, she later told the *Vassar Quarterly* reporter, "It never occurred to me to get into the arena. Rodeo was advertised as the world's most dangerous sport, and I believed that."

But she could not get the shots she was seeking so far from the ring, and she disliked using a telephoto lens because she thought the background got all "squished against the action."

She told *ProRodeo Sports News* in 1999, "I had to watch it behind the chutes [where] the guys would be pulling their britches down and things like that [to put on their padding before entering the arena]. But I knew so many of them as buddies that I was really just one of the guys. I wasn't trying to do anything but get a good picture."

According to Louise, "There really wasn't ever any plan to have women get in the arena. Because you can't say to someone in one breath that it's the world's most dangerous sport, and then the next thing you know you've got some dame out in the middle of the arena."

Yet she realized that if she wanted to make a career of rodeo photography, she would have to be inside the ring, closer to the action, and take her chances with charging bulls and bucking horses. She finally bolstered her courage to ask officials if she could shoot inside the ring.

In 1963 the Rodeo Cowboys Association issued Louise a pink press card, making her the first woman to receive permission to photograph action inside the rodeo arena. (In 1975 the association changed its name to the Professional Rodeo Cowboys Association—PRCA.)

In a 2012 *Inside Tucson Business* interview she said, "I was told I could get in the ring, but not to get in the way. If you get run over, that's too bad. So I learned pretty quickly not to get in the way."

Her status as the first woman photographer inside the arena caused a few raised eyebrows, but Louise always maintained, "I wasn't trying to prove anything." All she wanted was to take a good picture.

One of her first sojourns into the arena found her facing an arena boss who told her, "Get the hell out of the way and what are you doing in the arena, anyway?" "I wasn't exactly welcome," she told Betty Barr.

She had a lot to absorb about rodeo contests but was an avid student and quickly learned the intricacies of events that comprise most major rodeos. One of the first things she discovered was that saddle bronc riding is one of the more difficult competitions to photograph. As she tried to follow the horse's path, the bronc would sprint from one part of the arena to another, trying to dislodge its rider. The cowboy must not touch the horse with his free hand, and waving his hat is strictly forbidden. Timing is essential, as the rider has to spur the horse above the break of the animal's shoulder on its first jump out of the chute, and then try to stay on the irritated steed for what might seem like an eternity but in reality is only a matter of seconds. Balance and style are more important in bronc riding than brute strength.

Years later Louise recalled her experience photographing saddle bronc rider Allen Houston at the Tucson Rodeo:

His horse reared up in the chute, and went over backwards on him. This is why the so-called association saddle does not have a horn on it. If his saddle had had a horn, Allen would have suffered severe internal injuries—that horn would just about disembowel you.

I was standing out in front of the chute, taking a picture. As I saw this happening, I dropped the camera. I was so worried about him being killed that I didn't think to snap the shutter. Allen called me from the hospital later that night, and he said, "Did you get the picture?" I said, "No, I was too worried about you." "Fat lot of good that does me," he said. "I wanted to see what happened—what I lived through!"

Saddle bronc riding is in the rough stock category of rodeo events, which also includes bareback riding and bull riding. Since a bull can easily jump over or through almost any fence in its way, the rider must rely on timing, anticipation, and balance to keep the provoked creature on track, and in the arena, for just a matter of seconds.

An inner enclosure within the arena, called a turnback fence, is set up before this event to keep the steer confined to an area away from spectators, as it has a tendency to try and plow through anything—and anyone—that gets in its path. As a matter of safety, many cowboys at today's rodeos have abandoned their sweat-soaked cowboy hats in favor of helmets made specifically for bull-riding competition. Helmets are required attire at junior and intercollegiate rodeos.

Rough stock competitions demand balance and endurance, whereas timed events are based on skill and speed. Calf roping, team roping, barrel racing, and steer wrestling are the four events classified as timed activities. The cowboy is not only challenging his skill against other riders, but also competing with the clock.

The objective of calf roping is to lasso and tie a running calf as quickly as possible. The calf gets about a five- to thirty-foot head start before the cowboy starts his chase, flailing riata sailing through the air as he attempts to reel in the fleeing calf. The cowboy must then jump off his horse and grab the calf by its flank, toss it to the ground, and tie three of its legs. The calf must stay tied for six seconds. Louise soon found that trying to take a photograph of this split-second action was an athletic achievement in itself.

In team roping, two cowboys, one called a header and the other a heeler, must catch and rope the heels of a steer. The header lassos the steer by the horns, followed by the heeler tying the animal's back legs.

Team roping, or heeling, is "so fast," Louise said, "I actually have to push the camera's shutter before I see it take place; if I wait, it will be too late."

Steer wrestling, or bulldogging, is also a team event. The hazer keeps the steer on track, running in a straight line, while the dogger leaps on the animal, grabbing it by the horns and wrestling the five-hundred-pound beast to the ground, making sure it lands on its side with all of its feet pointed in the same direction.

Barrel racing is the only women's competition in PRCA rodeos. The cowgirl must maneuver her horse around a series of barrels in this timed event that usually sees the winner completing the course in less than twenty seconds. According to Louise,

In all events the stock is drawn by number from a hat. There are two judges who draw the stock for every contestant; they do this in front of the rodeo secretary, who makes sure that no rider competes on the same stock twice in a row. It is the luck of the draw: with some horses and bulls, no amount of riding talent and effort can make the rider mark high enough to win. In the timed events, how straight or how fast the animals run can make the difference—by seconds—that will mean a win or a loss.

As a photographer in the arena, my job is to record the action every time a chute gate opens—and never to get in the way. The worst thing for anyone working on the ground to do is interfere with the action: it's better to get run over—flattened—than to alter the movement of any animal. You soon

Billy Neal, 1963, Arizona Rodeo Association, Sonoita, Arizona
COURTESY OF SERPA PHOTOGRAPHY, L.L.C.

*learn where to be for the various events, and to keep an eye
on the nearest fence to climb—in case you need to get out in
a hurry.*

It did not take long for Louise to become proficient at gaug-
ing the speed and direction of these animals, all while trying to
get the best angle for the perfect image.

Her first year in the arena, she went wherever there was
a sanctioned rodeo, particularly in Arizona. She shot Arizona
Rodeo Association events in Casa Grande, Sonoita, and Sierra
Vista. She was at the Ajo rodeo that fateful day in November 1963 when President John F. Kennedy was shot. Officials
wanted to cancel the rodeo but since many of the contestants
were on the road already they dedicated the rodeo to Kennedy.

Jack Mulligan, 1964, Arizona Rodeo Association, Casa Grande, Arizona
COURTESY OF SERPA PHOTOGRAPHY, L.L.C.

That was also the year she photographed the rodeo in Boulder City, Nevada, that left her with a broken sternum and a few bum ribs after the bull flung her into the air and proceeded to stomp on her once she landed.

"The bull had weight," she told reporter Betty Barr, "and he was pushing me into the ground. When he threw me up in the air, that didn't hurt, but when I came down, that's when he proceeded to stomp me in the dirt."

"All I could think of was that my $600 camera would be ruined," she said in a 1967 interview with the *Arizona Daily Star*. "I saved the camera but broke two ribs."

In an interview years later, as Louise recalled that dreadful day that left her flat on her back, unable to get up, she said if a bull charged her again and aimed for her camera, "I'd hit him over the head with it."

Another time when she found herself in a dangerous situation, she lay on her stomach just inside the arena fence as bull and rider charged across the ring. This time she took the precaution of keeping her feet just under the fence on the chance she might have to scramble and roll under the boundary to get out of the charging bull's way.

"There's always a good chance of getting hurt," she told the *Arizona Daily Star* in 1967, "especially if you don't know enough to watch behind you every second you're in the arena."

The following year she was shooting rodeos in cities across Arizona, including Scottsdale, Chandler, Mesa, Casa Grande, and Sonoita. Of course, she was always in town to photograph the Tucson Rodeo. By this time she was shooting for the stock contractors as well as the cowboys.

Her life became a spiraling dust devil of vicissitudes. She was on the road almost every weekend, dragging her children with her from one rodeo to another. During the week when she had to be away, the girls were left with a bevy of babysitters.

In every town and at every rodeo, Louise looked for the familiar face of the one cowboy she could not forget. Lex Connelly had returned to the rodeo arena shortly after his stint with the Marine Corps was up. For eleven years he earned top spots in major rodeos across the country competing as a roper and steer wrestler. Retiring from the arena in 1957, he went on to manage San Francisco's Cow Palace and later served as an administrator with the Rodeo Cowboys Association, becoming an integral part of its growth. Lex was instrumental in obtaining nationwide television coverage for the National Finals Rodeo.

In 1960, when Louise was just starting her photography career, she apparently recommended to Lex someone he might want to hire at the RCA. In the last letter that survives between the former sweethearts, Lex thanks Louise for her hiring suggestion and briefly touches on their youthful liaison.

"After all these years," he wrote, "it's kind of strange to see you wind up in my old home country, but good to know you're there, too. No need going any farther into them there sort of thoughts. Just be happy in dear old Arizona. And, do think about a little jaunt to the Colorado rockies [*sic*] this summer. From now on the heat there'll keep this on your mind, and we'll be in touch later about the possibilities."

Possibilities did arise over the ensuing years, allowing Louise and Lex to rekindle their long-ago love affair. "When Lex was anywhere around," Louise told the Rodeo Historical Society, "I wanted to get a picture of him." If they were at the same rodeo, they would celebrate their reunion into the night, sometimes with other cowboys, sometimes alone, then go their separate ways in the morning—a ritual that continued for the next twenty years.

～～

As she was learning her trade and gaining the reputation as a fine rodeo photographer, Louise made the acquaintance of some of Arizona's more prominent movers and shakers who also had a love of rodeo.

Rancher Jack Goodman has been going to rodeos since 1936. For many years his family owned, among other buildings in Tucson, the Santa Rita Hotel, which was the preferred place to stay for visiting rodeo folks. In the early years, the rodeo parade ran through the middle of town, right by the Santa Rita. Marchers started on Scott Street, swung back to Sixth Avenue, headed down to the railroad tracks, and followed the tracks to Toole Avenue.

Jack is a founding member of the Mountain Oyster Club, an exclusive "members only" dinner group, to which Louise belonged for many years. Although the club changed locations several times, it originated in the basement of the old Santa Rita

Hotel. Jack met Louise shortly after she arrived in Tucson and they remained fast friends through the years.

"She was the last of the wild bunch," he says. "She did not live by anybody's rules." Jack, who at one time owned a cattle ranch in the mining community of Mammoth, about fifty miles north of Tucson, introduced her to other influential local citizens, and it may have been one of these individuals who invited her to the social gathering that left her attached to and encumbered by a rather large, amorous snake. Although the story cannot be substantiated, her daughter Lauren, who was a teenager at the time, remembers hearing about the evening from her mother.

The party was in full swing when Louise arrived at the get-together that warm summer evening, showing off her best assets in a long, low-cut, tight-fitting gown. Cast and crew from *The Addams Family* television show, which ran on the ABC network from 1964 until 1966, were filming in town and had been invited to the sunset soirée.

According to Lauren, someone in the *Addams Family* assemblage had brought along a rather large snake, most likely a boa constrictor that probably had been part of the recent filming. Daredevil Louise was drawn to the snake and soon had it wrapped around her neck.

As the evening progressed, the snake bored of the festivities and tried dozing around Louise's décolletage, but the noise of the party kept it awake. Before long it sought refuge down her dress and soon curled itself around her amble bosom.

Somewhat taken aback by the forwardness of the overly friendly reptile, Louise frantically tried to loosen its grip on her chest. She struggled and wiggled, but to no avail—the snake just cuddled up and tightened its grasp. Nothing would convince the ardent serpent to release its embrace of her lovely breasts.

With very little room to maneuver in the slim-fitting gown, she finally had to be helped into an adjoining room by several of the women at the party, who then tried to dislodge the snake. Eventually Louise convinced the now-satisfied, maybe smirking lothario to come up for air.

She put everything back where it belonged, smoothed down her dress, returned to the party, and had a great time for the rest of the evening.

Chapter 8

I pulled up my britches
and got out of there.

Louise made yearly visits back east to visit her mother and father (both had remarried). Her children loved these summer visits, particularly their time on the New Jersey shore, where Louise's father had a summer home. They tolerated their grandmother, even giving her the affectionate nickname "Moulie."

Between these annual vacations, however, Louise often found herself frantically flying to New York to rescue her mother from her latest crisis. Moulie frequently experienced bouts of extreme stress caused by excessive drinking. She would call her children (Louise, Anne, and Wendy), tell them she was going to kill herself, and expect them to drop whatever they were involved with and come to her aid. For Louise that meant finding a babysitter for her children, canceling whatever photography events she had scheduled, and racing across the country to be at her mother's side. Her first chore upon arriving was to confiscate the numerous liquor bottles her mother had hidden around her apartment.

Louise never got over her mother's disapproval of her life and the career she had chosen. "To Mother, a photographer took passport pictures," she said in the *Vassar Quarterly* interview. "She thought rodeo had no class at all." Moulie was ashamed of Louise's profession, even as Hollywood came calling on her daughter once again.

In 1965 *The Great Sioux Massacre* was filmed partly at Old Tucson Studios, originally built in 1938 and located just west of town. Joseph Cotten and Darren McGavin played the leading roles of Maj. Marcus Reno and Capt. Bill Benton, respectively, while Philip Carey portrayed Lt. Col. George Armstrong Custer. The movie certainly did not revolve around Louise's character, but she had a principal role at the beginning of the film. Cast as Mrs. Turner, wife of an Indian agent, Louise's character is captured by the Sioux. Custer convinces Crazy Horse and Sitting Bull that he will hang a multitude of their people if Mrs. Turner is not released. Fortunately for Mrs. Turner, she is eventually freed from captivity.

Her movie career ended with a small part in the 1967 film *Devil's Angels*, which was filmed near the southern Arizona town of Patagonia.

During her short film career, Louise continued to make the rounds of the rodeo circuit. Yearly calendars that she scrupulously maintained from 1965 until her death are filled with entries of rodeos she photographed in Mesa, Chandler, Casa Grande, Douglas, Willcox, Gila Bend, Florence, Sierra Vista, Prescott, Holbrook, Flagstaff, Globe, Kingman, and even Kearney, a small mining community in eastern Pinal County. And of course she was always available for Tucson's annual Fiesta de los Vaqueros, which has been a mainstay in the Old Pueblo since 1925.

"Cowboys are asked not to shoot up the town," read the headline in the *Arizona Daily Star* the day of Tucson's first rodeo, February 21, 1925 (the same year Louise was born). The small frontier town hosted what would become one of the best professional rodeos in the country. Prizes to be won that first year included a 750-pound block of ice, 100 pounds of potatoes, and a "Big Cactus" ham. Several thousand spectators watched the three hundred contestants vie for a purse worth $6,650. The Santa Rita Hotel hosted a dance on the eve of the rodeo attended by participants, tourists, and the town's leading citizens.

Today, the nine-day Fiesta de los Vaqueros boasts an arena capable of seating eleven thousand avid fans who have come to watch 650-plus cowboys and cowgirls compete for a purse of more than $420,000. The Tucson Rodeo Parade, which is viewed by more than two hundred thousand excited kids and parents, holds the title as the world's longest nonmotorized procession.

This was the electric atmosphere Louise grew to love year after year as she set about forging a reputation as a professional photographer in rodeo arenas across the state and throughout the Southwest. Her pictures captured the soul of rodeo, the good and the bad slices of life, the ups and downs, literally, of cowboy life both on and off the field. She absolutely loved the dirt and the dust and the heat, although she could do without the rain, snow, and sleet that sometimes accompanied a show. In this grimy, gritty, macho setting, she shot some of her most spectacular photographs.

Yet according to an interview Louise gave to the *Arizona Quarter Horse Journal* in 2011, "I didn't know anything about cameras; it was all hit and miss. I soon learned that if you overexposed, which I did constantly—I set (the camera) at 500 (shutter speed) and shot at 5.6 (aperture), and I just left it there. I didn't have time to change it in the arena, and very often, I was running round and I'd be shooting right into the sun."

She took one of her most famous shots at the Chandler, Arizona, rodeo in 1964. *Skeeter in the Dust* portrays a bucking bronc leaping several feet in the air while cowboy Roy "Skeeter" Humble struggles to stay on. And while the horse is defi-

Skeeter in the Dust, *1964, Chandler, Arizona Junior Rodeo*
COURTESY OF SERPA PHOTOGRAPHY, L.L.C.

nitely kicking up a heap of dust, there was an actual dust storm occurring at the moment she took the picture. She told *Cowboys & Indians* magazine, "We couldn't see him and so couldn't time the ride. We all fled for shelter until the dust settled." Very few rodeos are suspended because of inclement weather, but this was one of the few times a rodeo was cut short because of a perilous, sometimes deadly storm called a *jegos* by the early Pima Indians.

In March 1966 Louise headed north to photograph the Phoenix Jaycees' Rodeo of Rodeos at the city's newly built Arizona Veterans Memorial Coliseum.

Although average temperatures hover above one hundred degrees a good part of the year in Phoenix, that first week of

March was bitterly cold and wet. Some even reported seeing snow falling on giant saguaros that outlined the city. The coliseum had opened the previous November, but work was still progressing as the rodeo got underway.

Sloshing through the mud and muck around the arena, Louise did her best to get good shots, but a large body of water that had settled in front of the roping chutes made it difficult to know when a poor animal would get its footing and tear out the pen. Each day the puddle grew larger, finally becoming so big and annoying that the cowboys christened the giant pond Lake Okeechobee, after the largest freshwater lake in Florida.

This sadly soaked rodeo also acquired the title of the first underwater rodeo. One poor roper missed his steer completely as he tore out of the chute, and Louise captured him in midair just before he landed in the frigid, ever-expanding lake waters.

Rodeo clown Wick Path happened to be working this rodeo. Clowning since 1948, Wick was one of the best and most reliable clowns in the business. He knew his job was to protect, and sometimes save, cowboys who got thrown, and he is credited with rescuing more than one rider from certain death.

Wick and another clown, Jimmy Schumacher, who was "one of the funniest men ever to enter a rodeo arena," according to the ProRodeo Hall of Fame, both saw Louise go into the outhouse behind the chutes just before opening ceremonies. As soon as she had settled in, the two men started rocking the restroom facility back and forth as hard as they could, hooting uproariously as Louise tried to comprehend what was happening. Not knowing if she was in the midst of an earthquake or something just as dire, "I pulled up my britches and got out of there," she told the Rodeo Historical Society. Outside she found the two men doubled over and knew she had just been tested. Hoping she would not have to go through such a mortifying experience again, she prayed she had passed. She and Wick became fast friends through the years.

"Rodeo is a common denominator," she said in the *Vassar Quarterly* interview, "an equalizer. Cowboys don't give a tinker's damn whether you came from a rich family . . . or anything else as long as you're a real person. If they don't like you, they'll let you know it. That applies to all the West, not just rodeo."

Almost anyone who crossed paths with Louise became her friend, regardless of his or her profession, education, or upbringing. She accepted people as they were and welcomed their idiosyncrasies and differentness to her table.

She met Tucson painter and sculptor Ted DeGrazia around this time. DeGrazia's colorful images of southwestern scenes and Native American children endeared him to thousands of admirers around the world.

Louise photographed DeGrazia in 1966, focusing on his ruggedness, yet she also showed his softer side by taking pictures of his hands as he molded a clay sculpture. In a 2012 *Tucson Weekly* article about DeGrazia, reporter Margaret Regan said he was so pleased with the photographs Louise took of his rough, aged hands that he put one of the images on a card and sent it to her with the note, "To Louise! Let's Do a Book. Love, Ted."

DeGrazia once claimed he was "in competition only with myself, and that's tough, because I believe that each thing I do must be better in some way than the last." As Regan's story continued to delve into the relationship between these two artists, she suggested that in one of Louise's images of him, DeGrazia "seems to recognize that in Serpa, he's up against a force at least equal to himself."

Chapter 9

I am Louise Serpa.

Television game shows were big in the 1960s, and one of the most popular was *To Tell the Truth*, which ran from 1956 until it went into sporadic syndication from 1969 through 2002. Bud Collyer hosted a panel of four well-known actors, often Tom Poston, Kitty Carlisle, Orson Bean, and Peggy Cass. In 1967 Louise's unique profession made her the perfect contestant for the show.

The program included three contestants, all of whom claimed to be the central figure. Each was asked, "What is your name, please?" and each challenger answered with the same name—"I am Louise Serpa." The panelists had to figure out who was the real person by asking questions of all three challengers.

Louise headed for New York and appeared on the show dressed in snow-white jeans (something she rarely wore in the arena) topped by an orange long-sleeved shirt. Her hair, sans her usual western hat, was neatly coifed. The other two panelists were similarly dressed but sported no Levi's. The questions flew fast and furious to all the competitors. Louise was amazed how much the other two contestants knew about her life, both before and after she became a rodeo photographer, and commended the work they had put into memorizing her history.

She fooled Orson Bean and the audience, but the other three panelists guessed she was the real Louise Serpa. After the show she asked Kitty Carlisle what tipped off her identity. Kitty told her it was because she was the only one wearing jeans and she just looked like a Vassar girl. "Oh shit," Louise said, "I have tried to live that down all my life." For the wrong answers from Orson Bean and the audience, Louise and the other two contestants each won $200.

Back in Tucson by the time the television show aired, she and her girls headed out to watch the program on a friend's color television set, something Louise could not yet afford. Running late, she barely stopped her old station wagon at a stop sign and sure enough, a policeman pulled her over.

He appeared overly cautious as he asked for her driver's license, questioned where she was coming from, and proceeded to walk the entire perimeter of her car examining it from hood to trunk. He was particularly interested in the red stripe that ran around her vehicle. Seems an irate woman in a station wagon similar to Louise's that also sported a red stripe had recently walked into her husband's place of business and poured ice water over his head. What crime the man may have committed to warrant his spouse's action is unknown, but he filed suit against his wife, who apparently was hiding from authorities. Fortunately Louise was able to explain that she had no husband and had not recently poured ice over anyone. The officer let her go, and the threesome scrambled down the road, arriving just in time to see the show.

As expected, Louise's mother was not at all pleased that her photographer daughter was appearing on television brandishing her sordid profession before the entire country. She had asked Louise not to tell anyone what she did for a living, fearing her neighbors would snub her, but no one could stop her elite cronies from watching their favorite game show. At precisely one o'clock on the day of the show, even the elevator ceased running in the senior Louise's high-rise apartment building as everyone tuned in to watch *To Tell the Truth*, much to her mortification and humiliation.

◆◆◆

Starting in the early 1960s, Louise meticulously kept a yearly calendar of her photo assignments, including rodeos she was scheduled to shoot, cutting competitions, quarter horse shows, and polo matches. Some weeks she photographed up to five rodeos. Almost every weekend she was on the road with one or two jobs.

Along with detailing the demands of her business, these calendars provide a glimpse into her daily life: hair and nail appointments, dentist and doctor schedules, luncheons and parties, tennis and music lessons, car repairs, weddings and funerals, professional as well as personal trips, and the birthdays of her two growing daughters. Numerous dates are marked with theatrical shows, as she particularly enjoyed attending the opera and going to movies. She listed the day of the Super Bowl every year, along with special church masses such as a jazz or folk service. She kept track of heavy rainfalls, a welcome albeit rare event in Tucson, and recorded sales at Tucson's Steinfeld's department store. Through the years she tried several times to stop smoking, with her first attempt recorded on her calendar on May 1, 1969, followed by another attempt in 1974. Eventually she did manage to quit.

This diary of her daily tasks offers significant insight into Louise's professional and personal life, as well as that of her children.

Mia attended scout meetings and took piano, dance, and tennis lessons. On her eleventh birthday in 1967, Lauren clearly

Louise at polo fields, circa 1963–1964

COURTESY OF SERPA FAMILY

wrote on her mother's calendar that she wanted a surfboard and a guitar. She apparently got the guitar, as weekly lessons soon started appearing on the calendars.

By the late 1960s trips to Mexico showed up on the calendars as Louise headed south of the border to photograph rodeos in the northern copper-mining town of Cananea in the state of Sonora. She continued to shoot this particular rodeo for many years.

Her entries listing quarter horse shows flourished over time. This lucrative, welcome source of income kept her traveling from her favorite show in Sonoita to towns across Arizona, including Phoenix, Scottsdale, Winslow, Globe, Prescott, and Yuma.

Louise also found herself in demand to shoot polo competitions, another profitable undertaking for her.

Polo did not become popular in the United States until the 1870s, even though the sport has been in existence for over twenty-five hundred years. Great expense is involved in owning and training polo horses, and as the country suffered through wars and depressions, the game declined in popularity. The 1970s saw a resurgence of matches as corporations began sponsoring polo teams, bringing much-needed financial resources onto the field. Polo clubs were soon appearing across the country, dominated by eastern organizations but also spreading into Texas, California, and eventually Arizona.

Louise had retained an interest in polo from the time she first met Lex Connelly in 1943, since Lex had excelled on the polo field at the New Mexico Military Institute. In several of their letters to one another, the two discussed owning and running a team of polo ponies after they were married. Discouraging the idea, practical Lex knew the sport of polo required deep pockets, and he also suspected it would never be as popular as other athletic events.

Louise's pictures of swift-footed polo ponies, along with rodeo events, cutting competitions, and quarter horse races, soon began appearing on the covers and inside spreads of national publications such as *Western Horseman*, *American Quarter Horse Journal*, *ProRodeo Sports News*, *American Cowboy*, *Cowboys & Indians*, *Range,* and the journal published by the National Cowboy and Western Heritage Museum, *Persimmon Hill*. Her reputation as a sure-footed, sharp-eyed photographer was taking off as rapidly as a high-spirited steed.

Chapter 10

I was lucky not to have to wear a hat.

Accidentally lassoed around the neck by a team roper at the 1967 Tucson Rodeo, Louise yanked the rope from her neck just before it choked her. *All in a day's work*, she thought, as she gasped for air and rubbed the welts circling her neck, although she admitted this was one of the scarier moments in her career.

Routine was not a word in Louise's vocabulary. When she felt her life becoming too mundane and monotonous, she looked for a challenge. The Vietnam War was in full force at this time, and "rather than sit and do horse shows, I wanted to be a war photographer," she told the Rodeo Historical Society. "I wanted to be in there instead of sitting there. Somehow I couldn't connect with taking pictures of horses going over fences, doing things they really didn't want to do anyway. And what difference did it make to anybody?"

Her good friend Jack Goodman intervened before she acted on her latest chancy impulse.

In April 1970 Jack had a horse named Raccoon running in England's Grand National Horse Race. He asked Louise to go with him to the Aintree Racecourse near Liverpool and photograph his horse during the event. The melancholy she had been

England's Grand National Horse Race, 1970
COURTESY OF SERPA FAMILY

experiencing was replaced by wanderlust—she was thrilled to travel abroad again.

Often called the world's greatest steeplechase, the Grand National has run at Aintree since 1839, except for the few years it was canceled during both world wars and an unfortunate false start that aborted the tournament in 1993.

The grueling course is about two and one-quarter miles long, with horses running the entire distance twice. Sixteen fences, which are all jumped twice except for two (the Chair and Water Jump), challenge horse and rider at every hurdle. On the landing side of several of the fences, the ground is lower than on the ascent side, which the horse is unaware of until it is in the air and must quickly adjust to the difference in elevation. Conversely the Chair landing site rises higher than the ascent side.

Walking the grounds the day before the race, Louise decided she wanted to take photographs at two different jumps by running across the playing field as the horses made their way along the route. It did not take her long to realize the course was entirely too large for her to cover that much ground and still get the shots she wanted.

"All the photographers were in the end-field shooting head on," she told reporter Betty Barr, "and I didn't like that. You see more from the side. You can always tell the athleticism of a horse better from the side. I wanted to be standing in the brook that they would be jumping over."

She chose to shoot the Becher's Brook jump, which is about five feet up, six feet across, and six feet, nine inches on the downside, a hurdle referred to by some jockeys as jumping off the edge of the world.

In a 1995 interview with a Tucson television station she said, "I thought to get under it and shoot up at the horses coming [down] would be much more interesting than shooting them from the front or end-field."

No one had ever asked to be under a jump, much less right on the field, but Louise was determined to get in the best position possible. Asking officials if she could stay on the course to take pictures, and with Jack Goodman backing her up and praising her abilities with a camera, she received permission to enter the grounds.

"The English are wonderful," she told Barr. "They trust you. If you come out and say, 'Yes, I know what I'm doing' and act the part, they will let you do almost anything. They had never let a woman on the course before." Once again, Louise broke new ground.

When she wrote her article for the *Chapin School Bulletin* she said, "To my knowledge, I was the first woman allowed on the course and certainly the first person crazy enough to ask permission to photograph under the famed Becher's Brook jump."

The morning of the race dawned with a typical English forecast—gloomy, gray and rainy. She told *Zócalo* magazine, "It was cold as hell that day and I had to wear a dress because the Queen was there."

Pulling on a skirt, struggling to get her stockings up, and slipping into a pair of high heel shoes—certainly not what she was used to wearing to photograph horses racing around a field—she considered herself fortunate. "I was lucky not to have to wear a hat."

She loaded up her gear and slung two motor-driven Nikon cameras over her shoulder, one loaded with black-and-white film and the other with color. She kept a red strap around the camera holding color film so she could tell which camera to grab.

She found a good position at the Becher's Brook jump, the sixth jump in the race. Unable to see the horses coming, she could hear the ground pounding as the powerful mounts raced toward the fence. As soon as she saw the first horse clear the hurdle, she started shooting as fast as she could get her finger on the shutter, but she got very little usable footage. Twenty minutes later, the pack came toward her again. Of the twenty-seven horses that had started this dangerous, demanding race, only seven survived to the second round and now faced the grueling twenty-second jump. Again she waited until the horses broke over the fence before she began rapidly pulling the trigger on her camera. This time she was satisfied with her shots.

Huddling on the blustery, damp course with the other photographers, she had to wait over an hour before the race reached her vantage point. "Every year," she told *Zócalo*, "somebody . . . sends a bottle of scotch to the photographers since they had to wait so long in the cold for the jumps. They [the other photographers] looked at me and they looked at each other and they thought they could not hand me a bottle to swig out of, so I got a whole film canister filled with scotch." She kept the canister as a memento of her first Grand National.

As a thank-you gesture to her English hosts on this trip, Louise took pictures of people's cats and dogs to give them as house gifts. When she went back to shoot the race the next year, she was surprised how many more people wanted photographs of their pets. She now had a side job whenever she went to England.

On that second trip, so many of the photographers had seen the commanding prints Louise had taken while positioned underneath the fence, shooting just as the horses broke over the jump, that they all wanted to be on the course instead of safely several yards away.

From England Louise went to Ireland to photograph the Dublin Horse Show for *Chronicle of the Horse* magazine. This has been one of Ireland's best-attended horse shows for over 150 years. Thousands of people from all over the world come to watch some of the finest international jumpers. Again, no woman had ever photographed the Dublin show, but Louise was warmly accepted into this gentlemen-only event.

The next time she shot the Dublin Horse Show, she spotted a "wonderful, well-endowed Irish lass," carrying a brownie camera across the grounds, dressed in a T-shirt emblazoned with "Ohio State" across her bounteous bosom. A disturbing departure from Louise's first appearance in Dublin, but this was apparently the only credential now needed to get on the field.

Louise might not have felt the woman properly attired for the event, yet it was her own fortitude in knocking down stereotypical patterns of male-only photographers at athletic contests that opened the floodgates for women of all ages, and whatever modes of attire, to experience the thrill of getting the best shot of the day.

Surprisingly Louise's mother went with her to England and Ireland. In Ireland they were invited to visit a stud farm owed by the Aga Kahn, allowing Louise to "show Mother that once in a while the camera can get you somewhere with class" as she said in the Vassar article.

She delighted in telling the Rodeo Historical Society, "We went to all the parties before the race [in England] and over to

Ireland to meet the Aga Kahn, just to prove to her there was some class associated with photography, that it didn't need to be the grunge that she thought it was. She just thought that anyone who did photography was the bottom of the pit."

Shortly after mother and daughter had established a tolerable peace with each other on their jaunt to England and Ireland, Louise Yandell Barber Larocque Browne died on October 9, 1970. She was only sixty-seven years old but had lived a life dominated by drugs and alcohol for too many years.

Chapter 11

God help me at US Customs.

L ouise made several more excursions to photograph England's Grand National and the Dublin Horse Show. In the
summer of 1972, she took fifteen-year-old Lauren and thirteen-
year-old Mia on a jaunt around the British Isles. Although she
did not shoot the Grand National that year, she did make it to
Dublin in time to introduce her daughters to the intricacies and
talents of both horse and rider in the Irish competition.

Maintaining a journal of the trip, which lasted from July 3,
when they left New York, until they landed back in the United
States on August 10, Louise experienced all the angst, annoy-
ance, and amazement of any mother with two teenagers who
felt their own agenda superseded anything their prehistoric
mother had in mind. She wrote at the start of the journal:

*Having long since recognized my singular propensity for
cowardice, I know the only positive method of self-control is
to announce to the world at large that I'm going to do something and let shame keep me from backing off. My pronounce-
ment of last winter was to broaden the horizons of my two
unsuspecting teenage daughters by subjecting them to The
British Isles or vice versa. And to make it sound more impres-*

sive I declared, with unfounded conviction, that I would pho-
tograph the Dublin Horseshow. Hurrah! Somehow the actual
planning stage got itself bogged in a series of valid excuses
(procrastination is the technical word) until all deadlines con-
verged at once. A dangerous practice! . . .

To say that my intellectually inclined girls dragged their
feet all the way across the Atlantic is understatement. Neither
of them wanted to be "subjected to culture" during a vaca-
tion that obviously should be devoted to roller skating, riding,
boys, sailing, boys. Rather a horrifying challenge to a mother
armed only with their "best interests at heart."

Shopping at London's prestigious Harrods department store mollified the girls on their first day abroad. The next morning Louise steered them toward Westminster Abbey, then on to the Tower of London, where "the jewels almost sent Lori into orbit," before taking the hydrofoil to Greenwich and lunch at the seventeenth-century Queen's House.

As they waited outside Whitehall for the changing of the horse guards, "who should sail through the gates in a huge limo but the Queen Mother," Louise wrote. "She's beautiful!"

By the fourth day Louise was ready to let the girls venture out on their own. "Today was the day of the big experiment," she wrote, "the unleashing of my children on greater London." Apparently they did fine attending a movie then "tubing" home without incident. "Can you imagine allowing two attractive teenage girls to travel the New York subways & streets alone at night?"

The next day as they toured the London sights in a drenching rain (St. James's Palace, Trafalgar Square, Buckingham Palace), Louise advised, "Buy umbrellas, even if you do live in Arizona, and carry them without complaint. It doesn't really pour but it sure soaks."

Renting a car, the trio headed down the road for Cambridge, where they expected to stay at the Garden House Hotel but learned it had burned down three months prior. Finding a bed–and-breakfast ("clean and God knows cheap at £1 apiece with 25 pence for breakfast"), they rented a rowboat to sail down the Thames before heading to Bedford, Northampton, Leamington, and Warwick, where Louise found "the castle is the most beautiful so far. . . . Torture chambers, dungeons, the great Hall & bedrooms, an Elizabethan collection including her side saddle which Lauren loved remembering 'Elizabeth R' [the 1971 BBC television series]. A real feeling of age & history. We walked in peacock gardens and my pied-piper-ish child, Mia, disturbed the digestive tract of *every* peacock—flocks of them by feeding them peanuts. As we left, they followed in a swarm."

That evening their mail caught up with them, delivering disappointing news.

A waiting letter informed me I would not be allowed to photo-graph the action stills for an American TV series being filmed in Wales due to labor union restrictions. There went $150 per day!

We were asked to visit Madresfield Court in Malvern, Worcestershire County belonging to Lord and Lady Beau-champ. A beautiful estate; moat encircled mansion with flocks of Canadian Geese, ducks & swans; long avenues of incredible trees including a redwood, vistas, gardens and real evergreen maze, clipped 6 feet tall into which the chil-dren disappeared and were left floundering while we adults returned to cocktails . . . [which] were served in the library and we were joined by 2 other Lords & Ladies. I poked Mia and asked if she knew she was in a room with 4 lords. She only shrugged and said, "So?"

As they headed for Caernarfon, North Wales, the following day, Louise was sure she had taken the wrong road, as "eight miles seems eighty on these roads. One drives with the left hand constantly on the gear shift. We passed trucks where there was no room to pass. Lauren *belongs* in the back seat. Her shrieks scare me more than the traffic."

"The girls wanted beach, so we found our way out through a maze of high-hedge-rowed roads. Beach, as we know it, it wasn't. Smooth stones edged by freezing water. We sat shivering in sweaters while a few hardy Welsh idiots actually went swimming."

Just over two weeks into their vacation, they were off to Edinburgh the following morning. Louise noted that they had "gone just over 900 miles since Heathrow."

"10 am departure seems to be the best I can manage," she moaned. "The troops need whipping into gear each day to make breakfast and since it is included in the cost per night, I insist we get our money's worth. Gorgeous day again—verging on hot. It's a four hour drive through very different quite lovely country. Bigger hills, daisies, hedgerows of big trees."

In Edinburgh their adventures continued.

The zoo beckoned; we found a bus which dropped us at its gates. Fantastic zoo, really. With a panoramic view of the city, but all steeply built on a hillside—tough on old mothers with aching backs. In the aquarium building, we discovered a fish called a Serpa Tetra. Naturally I had to find the aquarium keeper, fish tender—what would you call him?—to point it out among the assortment in that tank. By then the girls were used to my talking to any & every stranger I could find.

We found the hyenas and proved to Lauren that her dog looked like a hyena—Bedlington terrier cross.

At the end of the day Louise noted, "Tomorrow is Lauren's 16th birthday, & all she wants is to be home to get her driver's license. I can't win."

July 21 dawned bright and sunny for her older daughter's birthday. "Shopped, bought kilts, sweater & a wallet. A new suitcase for Mia whose bag had disintegrated. Six rat-tail spoons and an antique pendant brooch for me. Expensive day but pleasing results."

The next morning dawned gray and drizzling as Louise headed out to find a launderette. She was delighted that not only could she wash two loads of clothes for 45 pence but the attendant refused to accept a tip for drying her laundry. Collecting her clean duds, she headed off to round up Lauren and Mia. "Today is *culpulsary* [sic] *culture* day!" she declared. "I will not be denied!"

A local dog show intrigued Louise but she had left her camera back at the hotel. "Some pro!" she wrote.

That afternoon,

The heavens opened up . . . Lauren's expensive Harrods's rain-proof coat was not [and] Mia had the inevitable thongs on her feet. Soaked, we lunched at Crawfords and sludged [sic] on up the hill to the [Edinburgh] castle. It was disappointing to me as castles go except for seeing the room where Queen Mary hatched James the VI. The view would have been spectacular had we been able to see it. Scottish mists! Lauren "split" and went back to the hotel, drenched & uncultured! Mia and I, thanks to her mad & insatiable desire for fudge, trudged down the Royal Mile to the palace, hitting the fudge shop near the bottom. (Bad fudge, incidently [sic]). Her appetite quenched, Mia obtained a modicum of culture and considerable moisture.

They were next off to the town of Aviemore, in the Scottish Highlands.

I've come to believe that the national game of all Britain is passing on the road where there is no room. I'm getting gradually gutsier about it but, oh Glory! . . . To pass the time driving, my eldest—Lauren—learned to whistle between her fingers amid gales of laughter. Mia read lying down, head under her coat because she claimed the passing trees made her car sick. She only surfaced when asked to read the map or to look at a lovely view. Typical Motherly cry—"I've brought you all this way to cover your head."

Traveling on to Inverness, she lamented that the last five days of rain was "too much for desert rats!"

But it lifted by 11:00 a.m. revealing the most fabulous view of the firth, Inverness and the mountains beyond. With the sun we set off to find pony-trekking and after 70 miles of circuitous driving, got Mia aboard a lackluster steed. Lauren and I drove along Loch Ness to kill the 1 1/2 hour time wait and discovered the [investigative] headquarters of the Loch Ness monster. Fascinating! Mia—typical of 13 year olds, blew a tizzy when she found out she'd missed that.

On July 26 they drove to the Isle of Skye, touted as "a place where time means nothing, and beneath every footstep lies five hundred million years of history." Lauren and Mia soon discovered nightly ceilidh (pronounced KAY-lee) dances at the Dunvegan Hotel, where they were staying. According to Louise:

A Ceilidh—is by definition a party, a dance, a sing-song. We watched the country dancing rather longingly—such fun and nothing really like it in the states—square dancing is akin but there are so many rather complicated individual pair dances as well . . . some speeded up variations of the minuet. The Scots do it with joy, agility and abandon—all ages!

John and his son Geoffrey Qunning, co-lodgers at the MacDonalds [the MacDonalds were the proprietors of the Dunvegan Hotel], were there. John bought me the local drink combination—a neat shot of (scotch) whiskey in one hand and a half pint of lager in the other—WOW. In this country it would floor me but perhaps you dance off the effects there. In any event I remained sober—surprisingly. Geoff asked Lauren to go to a larger ceilidh in Portree which lasted till 2 am. Not to be a kill-joy and like a fool, I said yes, and then "squirmed the bed" until they came safely home at dawn—2:30 am The daylight lingers until 11:30 pm and starts again so early—we could not get used to it.

The next night they went to another ceilidh at the nearby Misty Isle Hotel.

The "entertainment" proved to be the same group we saw in Inverness. They recognized us and proceeded to give us a wild evening—all of us doing Scottish dances. Total strangers came up and swept us in, never in a rude or harsh way but wanting us to enjoy ourselves as much as they themselves did. Lori must have danced with at least 8 different boys and ended up doing the steps very well. Mia was shyer and finally she asked our friendly drummer in the band—Bobby—whether or not they played rock. The joint fairly flew apart with their unleashed energy. We danced till the end at 1 am—I, without my brace and terrified lest the back give way. It didn't and I feel tired but the better for the exercise. I need about four nights sleep in a good bed, alone and asleep by 9:00! Never mind—this is exactly what I had prayed would happen on this trip and on the ideal level—involvement with people doing things their way and having fun.

With the girls sleeping in the next morning, Louise caught up with her hostess, Mrs. MacDonald, who "keeps us knee deep in tea and scones. Mia, I think, would be happy if she never had anything else to eat!"

That afternoon, the threesome went to Portree, the largest town on Skye. Along the way "we found a fantastic pottery shop where I went berserk and bought the most expensive wall hanging creation they had. Cashed a travelers check while they wrapped my acquisition in flocks of excelsior and stuffed it in a Grant Liquor box to take with us. God help me at US Customs."

On the Isle of Skye the Dunvegan Show is one of the most popular events of the year, and Louise looked forward to photographing the sheep and horse judging, sheep shearing and sheep dog exhibitions, plus a variety of children's events. But the day started out windy, dark, and cloudy, "ruining the chance of good color pictures," she lamented.

Skye is home to the MacLeod clan, who maintain Dunvegan Castle, built in the ninth century and the longest-occupied house in Scotland. Dame Flora MacLeod bestowed the honors at the end of the competition, something Louise said she would not have missed for anything.

The Grand Finale, and cold through to the marrow I wouldn't have stayed for any other, was Dame Flora MacLeod . . . gracious, sharp and humerous [sic] awarding the prizes.

Having come [to Skye] for one and stayed eight days . . . we bid adieux to the MacDonalds and drove sadly to the ferry. . . . Arrived in Ardlui [Scotland] at 4 pm barely in time to get the last room . . . lovely airy big room overlooking Loch Lomond with three beds. The drive today was possibly the most dramatic scenery of the whole trip; lakes, mountains, waterfalls and always the incredible reforestation projects. Some of the young pine and fir forests are 20 feet tall already. The hills look like a giant comb had worked on them.

Lauren was sad but in control until I made the mistake of playing the Skye Boat Song—"Speed bonnie boat like a bird on the wing . . ." and that reduced her to immediate tears. In her whole life she has never loved a place as much as Skye. Mission accomplished!

A quick drive around Loch Lomond, before it was time to return to Ireland.

Over the Erskine bridge to the Glasgow airport. I dumped the bags at Aer Lingus who were only holding 2 reservations for us. Typical! That was righted after standing in line. Then they sprung a 50 pence per airport head tax on me and wouldn't take a traveler's checque [sic]. Back upstairs to the bank, down and requeued only to find that the ticket agent couldn't change a £5 note. Up to bank again, queue down again, queue, finally bags weighed, tickets done. The girls parked in a no parking zone were happily watching a car which had gone out of control and impaled itself on a fence just behind us. Turned our car in to Godfrey Davis Inc.—we'll miss the little friend—a red Ford Cortina—which took us 2200 miles safely for £140 ($345.00).

The takeoff from Glasgow "was bad enough," according to Louise, but the landing even worse, with the pilot stopping two feet from the landing ramp. "So our first step on Irish soil was accomplished by disembarking down the tail stairs, walking on the apron and up more stairs to the ramp. I began to wish I hadn't bought the pottery in its Grant Liquor box, the walking stick, and was ready to jettison all cameras and umbrellas, as the back began to creak ominously!"

With only two days left in their trip, Louise made her way to the Dublin Horse Show grounds.

With only slight deviations found parking, the office for my credentials which were all in an addressed envelope awaiting my arrival. Thence to the Press room for a badge—leather yet!—which got me into the jumping enclosure. There is no such thing as one official photographer but we were all pretty well screened. Several German girls with instamatics snuck in only to be escorted out. The jumps, turf all were immaculate. Tremendous imagination and care. Flowers, potted plants at all jumps. The enclosure is the size of a polo field all turf, even the banks jumps, bordered by rounded clipped box hedge with deep beds of snapdragons, lobelia and marigolds in perfect bloom. Each individual I met, official or otherwise, was kind, considerate and helpful. (Not "nasty rude & inconsiderate," a peg I continually hung on my offspring.) We were drowned several times during the afternoon. Come the finish I was soaked, kinky-haired and back-achy. A big fat steak at the Hideout [Irish pub] fixed that and then while the girls went bump-carring at their carnival, I stayed and drank with Qwinn Dyer and his super 78 yr. old mother from Kilkenny.

She was back at the show the next day. "Shot some color of the International jumping. Pity the British team didn't come but they'd been threatened by the IRA and couldn't risk it before the Olympics. Had to play the apertures like a yoyo as the sun kept coming in and out."

On August 10 the entourage boarded the plane back to New York and Louise's journal entries end: "Perfume and hooch and cigarettes at Shannon. $17.95 for a quart of Scotch and 5 cartons. WOW."

Chapter 12

It never occurred to me that I was breaking some kind of barrier.

As rodeo and horse magazines continued to display Louise's strong, impressive photographs on their covers, her reputation as a photographer with a great eye for action and detail increased with each issue. In the early 1960s *Hooks and Horns* was the first publication to exhibit her art on its cover, while throughout most of the 1970s, the National Cutting Horse Association Annual Edition of its rule book presented its members with one of Louise's fast-action cover shots.

With her reputation as an exciting, exacting, and reliable photographer expanding, she was often out of town throughout the week, away from her children, missing events and occasions that were important to her daughters. She was sometimes not there when they needed her the most.

On February 16, 1973, fourteen-year-old Mia spent a good part of the day at the stables where she boarded her horse. She and a girlfriend planned to spend the night at Mia's house even though her mother was on the road. (According to her calendar, Louise was at a rodeo in Phoenix.) The two teenagers asked another girl at the stables for a ride home.

The winter weather that day was typical for Tucson, a cool sixty degrees with no unusual conditions that might affect their drive. Even the wind was calm, barely moving the tree limbs that dotted their drive as the little Volkswagen made its way along Oracle Road. Mia sat beside the driver while her girlfriend took the backseat.

As they made the turn from Oracle Road onto Orange Grove Road, they did not see the truck until it slammed into the passenger side of the vehicle.

"I ended up eating the windshield," Mia remembers, "cutting my lips badly." The driver cut her tongue on the steering wheel and the backseat passenger suffered a cut on her head. "Everyone went home that night except me. I was in the hospital for three days."

Every mother knows the heartrending, stomach-turning feeling of not being there when her child is sick or hurt. The two-hour drive from Phoenix to Tucson that Louise made that night to get back to her daughter must have seemed endless.

At age nineteen it was Lauren's turn to end up in the hospital. "I had gallstone surgery," she recalls, "plus they removed my appendix and I had tumors in my stomach as well. Back then they cut you all the way across your stomach. I was hospitalized for two weeks and then bed rest for a month." She says she still has her gallstones, "at least the ones they could fit in a bottle."

Of course Louise had her own physical problems through the years. Avoiding charging horses and bulls for a living had its ups and downs, as evidenced by the bull-stomping episode in Boulder City, Nevada, in 1963 that left her with a broken sternum along with several fractured ribs.

In 1972 she was hospitalized for the recurring back problems that had plagued her on the European trip with her daughters. She finally consented to disc surgery to relieve the constant pain. For two weeks she was stuffed into a contraption that rotated her body every half hour. No painkiller existed at the time that could ease the agony of this tortuous apparatus. Looking to her underage daughters for her own brand of relief, she had them smuggle her favorite tequila into the hospital, which seemed to help more than any drugs she was given.

By 1975 Louise was back in the swing of her demanding career, this time flying off to Australia, courtesy of *Life* magazine, to photograph the Sydney Royal Easter Show. This event, Australia's largest, brings in around nine hundred thousand people every year. "I was a good horse photographer," she told a *Tucson Citizen* reporter in 1997, "and they needed one, so I got handed the job. It never occurred to me that I was breaking some kind of barrier." Louise is considered the first woman to photograph the event.

The Royal Easter Show is called a celebration of Australian culture, featuring agricultural and animal competitions, carnival entertainment, and a bevy of traditional events, some of which date back to the first show in 1823, all organized by the nonprofit Royal Agricultural Society of New South Wales. Louise was so taken with the country that she returned in 1981 and 1985 to photograph the distinctive, unique animals and incredible people she met as she traipsed around the countryside.

Amateur as well as seasoned photographers sought out Louise to teach them how to shoot exciting, publishable rodeo pictures. *Life* magazine asked her to show color photographer Carlo Bavagnoli how to shoot rodeos. She took him to events in Scottsdale and Phoenix, directing him how to shoot and where to stand so he did not interfere with the action, particularly during calf-roping events. She told him not to move once in the arena, as the calf would see the movement and dodge to one side, probably eluding the rider's lasso.

Carlo listened and said he understood everything Louise told him. Unfortunately, the first time he got in the ring to shoot, he forgot all her instructions.

World-champion team roper Dale Smith had just set up to rope his calf when Carlo suddenly appeared in the arena. In a split second the calf spotted Carlo's movement and dodged Dale's lasso, the slack rope falling empty to the ground. In another split second Dale dismounted, grabbed Carlo, and smacked him across the face, a fineable offence in the rodeo ring. Mounting his horse, Dale rode to the office to report himself and pay his fine—no better money spent, he probably thought.

Chapter 13

You can't outrun a bull.

By the early 1970s Louise and her daughters felt the crunch of living in a too-small house close to the middle of town. One situation that might have pushed her into searching for more land and a larger house was the day Mia, home on break from college, woke up to find her mother cooking a rather large breakfast. Since Mia did not eat breakfast, it seemed like a lot of food for one person. Before long Lex Connelly sheepishly appeared, well rested and ready to chow down. Since Mia had been entertaining that evening also, it was a foursome that sat down to a rather uncomfortable meal before they all headed out the door to their respective appointments. It was time to get more space!

Louise wanted land, lots of land, and a house that could accommodate all of them without their stepping on each other. She purchased forty acres from cattle rancher Henry W. Jackson, property that sat at the foothills of the Rincon Mountains bordering Saguaro National Park, surrounded by stark wilderness, almost twenty-five miles from town. She was also within spitting distance of the underground magnificence of Colossal Cave, an area first inhabited around AD 900 by farming Hohokam Indians. It would be several years before she moved into her new residence on the X9 Ranch, a home of almost four thousand square feet that she designed herself, from the brick and sand adobe walls to the exposed beams on the vaulted ceilings.

"I had the land for seven years before I built the house," she said in a 1985 *Tucson Lifestyle* interview, "and I knew what I wanted."

She measured the length, width, and height of every window to obtain the best possible view. She selected floor tiles the color of the desert and ceiling beans from Mt. Lemmon pine trees. She painted every wall, door, and ceiling herself and had a fireplace built into every room.

In her bedroom she had a custom desk built at the head of her adobe and granite bed with a wall of bookcases behind her. A darkroom was off to one side, large enough to hold the thousands of negatives and prints she had accumulated.

She brought in a baby grand piano and placed it prominently in the living room. Her love of singing lasted throughout her lifetime, and according to her daughters, she sang almost every day whether she had an audience or not. "She sang in the choir, in the darkroom, in the car, at dinner parties," Mia confirms. "She was awesome!"

Louise ordered doorknobs for the ranch, an iron one shaped like a praying mantis and another resembling a scorpion that would latch the door leading to a patio that ran the length of the house. On the day the doorknobs were to be installed, she still had rollers in her hair when the worker arrived. To her amazement, the worker turned out to be actor Lee Marvin, a friend of the iron maker. He wanted to meet the person who had thought up such unique designs for her doorknobs.

"Once I got to the West Coast," Louise's now-grown half sister Anne remembers, "I would go and see her. One of my sister's many talents was to be beautiful in the execution of her living place. All of her houses were lovely. Each one got progressively more grand."

What Louise sought to create was a place where she could work, develop her pictures, put her feet up at the end of the day, and enjoy a refreshing glass of tequila.

In 1976 she moved into her new home, where she would remain for the next twenty-five years. Eventually she doubled her original forty acres, remodeling another home that sat on the property and adding a negative-edge swimming pool.

The trip to Tucson took a little longer, but Louise never minded the drive from her new home, located in the little community of Vail east of downtown Tucson, even though one night she hit a bull on this lonely stretch of road. She jammed her hands on the steering wheel, the incident totaled her car, and she discovered a large bump on her forehead later that evening, but she was back on the road the next day, headed for the Tucson Rodeo.

Louise was now the preeminent photographer at quarter horse and cutting shows throughout Arizona, as well as an integral figure at the Tucson Rodeo. The cowboys, announcers, stock contractors, and audience all looked for her presence in the arena. Even the rodeo clowns kept an eye on her, not wanting to get in the way of her shot, sometimes not an easy task to accomplish.

Charles "Chuck" Henson clowned at the Tucson Rodeo for years, meeting Louise in the 1960s. Chuck also hired on as a stuntman for several movies that were shot in and around Old Tucson Studios, just west of town. Both his mother and aunt, Marge and Alice Greenough, were famed saddle bronc riders during the 1930s and '40s. Rodeo surged through his blood. He was awarded for his clowning expertise in 1995 by induction into the National Cowboy Hall of Fame, with Louise attending the ceremony. Chuck retired from the ring in 1980, but he still has vivid memories of an incident that landed him on top of Louise during one bull-riding event.

Rodeo clown Chuck Henson
COURTESY OF SERPA FAMILY

It was sometime in the 1970s, Chuck recalls, when the rodeo was using a large, rolling wire turnback fence to contain bulls within the arena and away from spectators, instead of the smaller, sturdier fences that are used today. Chuck was toying with a high-horned bull, working it around a barrel and making a pass at it. He must have made the animal mad, because before Chuck knew it, that bull was right behind him as he ran for safety outside the fence.

He did not make it before the bull caught up with him and knocked him into the fence, tearing the screening down as clown and bull tumbled over each other. Beneath him Chuck heard the muffled cries of Louise. "Get off of me," she yelled, but poor Chuck could not move. "I can't," he shouted. "There's a bull on me."

Louise's version varies little from Chuck's:

Bulls are very agile. You can't outrun a bull. But if you just take a deep breath, and realize that the bull can't turn as fast as you can, then you have more control. So if a bull is coming at you, you wait until he's almost on top of you, and then you step aside or move forward past him.

The only time I ever put that theory to the test, I had absolutely no control over it at all. I'd like to say I was brave. The bull charged the turnback fence, which I was lying under, shooting up into the bullring. It actually charged Chuck Henson, the clown, and caught him around the back at the waist, bruising his kidneys. The bull mashed him into the fence with such force that the fence broke, and it was held up in place by a two-by-six and a base. The two-by-six broke and fell on my head. So there I was, lying on the ground with this fence on top of me. The bull went across the fence, and then turned around and came back at me. I didn't have a prayer, because I was practically out cold, down on the ground. So I waited until the last minute, and then just flipped over, and by that time, they had gotten a rope on the bull and got him away.

One of the judges, Jack Buschborn, came back in the office afterwards. I was sitting with a big banana-shaped bump on the side of my head from this thing, and he said, "That was pretty cool—to be able to lie there and just move at the last minute." I said, "Cool? I was out cold!"

In the end, Chuck says, "all Louise wanted to know was if her camera was all right."

Chapter 14

I am? It is? You are? We will?

By now Louise could afford more than one camera, and her repertoire of equipment increased along with her income. She had a 2 ¼ camera for a while that gave her larger negatives (two and a quarter inches square) and sharper images, but she found herself changing out the film too often since the camera held only twelve exposures compared to the thirty-six shots she could get with a 35 mm. Sometime in the late 1970s or early 1980s, she acquired her first motor drive just as these drives were becoming permanent components of cameras, allowing for multiframe shooting instead of one shot at a time.

Throughout her career Louise preferred Nikon cameras. "I started with them," she said, "because I could break them down pretty well myself, to clean and blow out and get a Q-tip in, just to keep them moderately clean. You're under terrible circumstances in the arena, and you're changing film in the dust all the time."

When she decided to start shooting color, she took a seminar at the Los Angeles College of Design, and although the school wanted her to teach a session on action photography, she declined the offer. Her class professor had her shoot one roll of color film—thirty-six exposures—with just one model as her subject. Louise thought she did a terrific job and had some wonderful pictures to show her instructor. He found fault with every photograph she took. It was a "very humbling experience," she said, "but I learned a lot."

According to Louise, Frenchman Henri Cartier-Bresson (1908–2004) was the best black-and-white photographer. Considered the father of modern photojournalism, he mastered the candid shot and was instrumental in developing what is called "the decisive moment" in photography.

Self-taught nature photographer Eliot Porter (1901–90) was her favorite color photojournalist. His images of Arizona's little-known Glen Canyon, taken in 1960, were turned into the book *The Place No One Knew* in 1963 with the hope that his intricate and vibrant landscape portrayals would influence President Lyndon B. Johnson, Secretary of the Interior Stewart Udall, and members of Congress not to flood the canyon to create Glen Canyon Dam. The effort failed, however, and Glen Canyon was buried under millions of acre-feet of water, its beauty lost forever.

Louise returned to Australia to shoot the Royal Easter Show in the early 1980s accompanied by daughter Mia. She would make one more trip to Australia in 1985 to capture the vividness of the wild yet sophisticated beauty of this incredible land.

Her schedule at home increased rapidly, with shows throughout the week as well as every weekend. Along with shooting the Maricopa Cutting Show, which allowed local competitors to show off their horses' abilities at working and controlling calves, she was taking advertising pictures for a local horse breeder. She contracted with a company in Berlin, Germany, to have some of her images displayed on buses as they moved about the town, giving her far more exposure than she had ever experienced. Rodeos, however, still commanded most of her time.

Prescott, Arizona, claims the title as having the oldest professional rodeo that offers cash prizes, with its first "cowboy contest" held July 4, 1888. The early participants were usually local cowboys and ranchers who competed on a roped-off tract of land to keep their horses from running off after unseating an unsuccessful rider.

In the early 1980s the Prescott Rodeo, along with the Calgary Stampede in Alberta, Canada, held the only wild horse races as part of their competitions. Calgary also had competitive chuck wagon races. Four horses were hitched to each chuck wagon, with four wagons racing around the track at one time. Obviously impressed with the drivers as she shot the chuck wagon races, Louise described these rugged characters as "canny, shrewd, and very, very aggressive."

Of course she was on hand for the Tucson Rodeo every February, and still shot junior rodeos whenever she could squeeze in one. She also continued her commitment to shoot Southern Arizona International Livestock Association events. No wonder she needed so many cameras!

She liked to attend the Cowpunchers Reunion held in northern Arizona at the end of each summer. The competitors were usually seasoned ranch hands who were not members of the PRCA. According to Louise, "The events are markedly different from those in regular rodeo arenas. When I shot the show in 1983 [held in Williams, Arizona, that year], they were not using bucking chutes. Saddle broncs were held between two mounted men (called snubbers) in the middle of the arena. Fathers held calves while their sons were dropped aboard to ride as far as they could. It was the epitome of old-time rodeo and friendly competition."

In the fall of 1982 she held the first exhibit of her work at Tucson's historic Arizona Inn, founded in 1930 by Arizona's first US congresswoman, Isabella Greenway. Her photographs caught the eye of then US secretary of commerce Malcolm Baldrige.

Secretary Baldrige, an avid rodeo participant successfully competing in team roping competitions since he was old enough to work as a ranch hand, wrote to Louise complimenting a photograph she had taken. He did not mention where the picture was shot, but it might have been at the Tucson Rodeo that year, and it may have been of him. "The photograph you took at Tucson is one of the best I have seen," he wrote, "because it really explains to the unitiated [*sic*] how to throw a heel rope." (In team roping, the two cowboys are called the header and the heeler.)

That October he sent her an article that had been written about her and again praised her work. "Anyone who can made [*sic*] a second-rate heeler look like a World's Champion, as you did in that great shot at Tucson, deserves the best."

Baldrige served as secretary of commerce from January 20, 1981, until he was killed in a rodeo accident in California on July 25, 1987. The horse he was riding in a calf-roping event fell on him. He was named Professional Rodeo Man of the Year in 1981 and inducted into the National Cowboy Hall of Fame in 1988.

It may have been those pictures hanging in the Arizona Inn that brought Louise to the attention of another man who would influence her career for years to come.

Louise felt fortunate to show her photographs at the famous inn. Sophisticated and cultured visitors from around the country stayed at this fashionable desert retreat, including fashion photographer Bruce Weber, who arrived in town to shoot a spread for *Vogue* magazine. Weber had already established himself as an advertising photographer for such well-known manufacturers as Calvin Klein, Ralph Lauren, Abercrombie & Fitch, Revlon, and Versace. Along with *Vogue*, his work has appeared in a variety of trendy publications, including *Vanity Fair, Elle, Life, GQ, Interview,* and *Rolling Stone.* After a day of shooting he had taken his whole crew to dinner at the Arizona Inn.

When he saw Louise's rodeo photographs displayed around the inn, he was so taken with the vivid action of the shots and the obvious passion the photographer showed for this type of work that he asked the manager if he might meet the person who had taken these remarkable images.

"I get a call at 11 o'clock that night," Louise said in her Rodeo Historical Society interview. "I didn't have a clue as to who he was. I had never heard the name. I had never seen the name. And he said he was here to do a shoot and wanted to come out and see my portfolio. Well I didn't have a portfolio. I never even thought about having a portfolio. If a picture was good it sold!"

She was on her way to Phoenix to shoot a rodeo and told Weber she would not be back until the wee hours of Monday morning. Bruce was supposed to leave town on Sunday, but he agreed to stay over and meet with her later on Monday.

Making the long trek to Vail and down the four-mile dirt road to the X9 Ranch house, Bruce was surprised to be greeted by a strikingly beautiful woman dressed in a long black skirt. She had pulled her hair back, he now recalls, saying, "With that smile, you couldn't help but fall in love with her." He sat enthralled for hours going over her work.

By this time Louise had figured out that Bruce photographed the Ralph Lauren and Calvin Klein ads, but she was still uncertain what he wanted from her.

"We talked for a bit and he saw what I had," she said, "which wasn't much. . . . The whole time he was talking to me, he was saying, 'You have to come to New York. You have got to meet So and So. And you are this and you are that.' And I kept saying, 'I am? It is? You are? We will?'"

Louise deemed Bruce "one of these extraordinary men who is always interested in any kind of talent that is new to him." And he will do anything in his power to help that individual if he feels his efforts will be worthwhile. Meeting Bruce, she said, opened up so many doors for her.

"I ordered some prints from her," Bruce remembers, "and fell head over heels in love with them."

He insisted she have a show in New York. She must hire a dealer to handle her work. And she certainly had to get a book published of her incredible athletic images.

"There is no way in the world I would have gotten outside my limited sphere if it hadn't been for Bruce," she told the *Fort Worth Business Press*. "I was good at what I was doing, but nobody outside of the rodeo ring would've known it."

As their friendship grew and Bruce introduced her to prominent individuals in the art and publishing industry, she soon found herself featured in *Interview* magazine. *People* did a spread on her in which she admitted she still dried her prints using an old hairdryer. "The rodeo is like a shot of adrenaline," she said in this interview. "Once in your blood, it never leaves you. . . . It's one of the few places where you can be taken at face value. It's not just the call of the wild. It's the whole combination of horses and freedom that I love."

"I have never seen it too windy, too dirty, too cold, too dangerous for her," said one cowboy about Louise.

Bruce arranged for her to have an exhibit of her photographs at a New York City art gallery. He even used her as a model "when he needed old age and wrinkles," said the then almost sixty-year-old and still attractive Louise. He photographed her for *British Vogue* as well as *New Mexico* magazine.

"She is a remarkable-looking woman," Bruce said in an 1984 *Arizona Republic* article. "Her life and feelings really show on her. She lives this really courageous lifestyle and it shows. I just thought she was very beautiful." And, according to Bruce, if she did relate the tale about the boa constrictor wrapping itself around her breasts in the 1960s, it was probably factual. "Any story she ever told about a snake was true," he said.

She became a fixture at his Montana ranch for weeklong stays along with an assortment of artists from a variety of genres. On one of these occasions she met Ingrid Seshi, then head of *Art News* and a feature writer for the *New Yorker* magazine. Louise had brought along several of her photographs as a thank-you gift for Bruce. Once Ingrid saw her photography, she became intrigued with the intricacy of Louise's pictures as well as the life of this former New York socialite who lived with her nose in the dirt and her eye glued to a camera. Ingrid wrote an article about Louise's fascinating career for the *New Yorker* and recommended a book of her work be published. Within two weeks a publisher called to discuss the possibility of producing a book of her rodeo pictures.

Her fame was also spreading around the rodeo circuit. In 1982 *ProRodeo Sports News* and Frontier Airlines awarded her a gold and silver trophy buckle for the best action photograph of the year. She was so proud of this award that she blushingly admitted to a *Western Horseman* reporter, "I wore it to bed the first three weeks I had it." In an interview over twenty years later she said she was getting so fat it was hard for her to wear the buckle properly. "I look at team ropers who have their buckles underneath their tummy, and that's about where mine is now," she told the Rodeo Historical Society.

Under Bruce's tutelage, as well as with recognition as one of the best rodeo photographers in the business, Louise found herself busier than ever. She worked her way through China in early 1982, taking photographs on a very tight, extremely structured agenda. She said she always wanted to go back and photograph China at her own pace, not according to someone else's schedule. She delighted in the Chinese people, whom she found kind and dignified, their interest in her work completely genuine. She applied these same attributes to rodeo people.

Upon returning home she traipsed across Arizona's desert floor to shoot a slew of rodeos from June through October, and then headed to Egypt that November to photograph about twenty cities in just under a month's time.

The pace she kept would exhaust even the fittest athlete. But Louise knew that every time she saw a new country or shot a different subject she was learning on the job, "always working over my head technically but always learning—always challenged, never bored."

She returned home in time for the beginning-of-the-year rodeos and cutting shows, but stopped long enough in June 1983 to have surgery on a nagging case of diverticulitis. Only six days out of the hospital, she headed for Prescott to shoot the Prescott Frontier Days Rodeo.

Louise would be the first to admit she suffered her share of injuries through the years. "Very often," she said, "I'll come out of the arena, and I'll be dripping blood from a hand or a shin or something, and I don't have a clue how it happened. It didn't hurt at the time, and I'd been concentrating too hard to pay attention."

That year in Prescott, however, she remembered every bump and bruise she acquired.

The horse would not stand still as it waited to be released from the bucking shoot. Its rider was both eager and anxious to grab the mount and start his ride across the arena to victory.

Louise stood just outside the gate as the horse came barreling out of the chute, hitting the gate and smashing Louise between fence and gate. She scrambled up the fence to avoid another hit but was too late. The horse smashed against her again, injuring a couple of her ribs, breaking her glasses, and worst of all, damaging her camera equipment.

Daughter Mia was on this trip and saw the frightening scene unfold. She rushed to help Louise, who was visibly shaking as she crossed the ring. Dazed and sore, she would have no part of leaving the rodeo. "Just shut up and go get me some tequila," she told her concerned daughter, then proceeded to shoot the remainder of the day. She was also on hand for the evening performance, black-eyed and bruised a deep purple from head to toe, still carrying her heavy, cumbersome cameras, but she had no intention of leaving before the show concluded. She was back in the arena the next day.

Chapter 15

My job is to capture that moment.

"Lex Connelly Killed in Airplane Crash," read the April 18, 1984, *ProRodeo Sports News* headline. "Former Rodeo Cowboy Association executive director Lex Connelly was killed April 5 when his light plane crashed into a hillside near Baker, Or. Connelly was enroute [*sic*] to Spokane, Wa, where he was to announce the Diamond Spur rodeo."

Fifty-eight-year-old Lex and his wife, Shirley, were alone in the single-engine Beechcraft Bonanza plane when it went down outside of Baker, Oregon. The weather report had called for heavy rain in the area that day with ground temperatures in the mid-forties. The cause of the crash was listed as iced-over wings. The two were buried in Fresno, California, where they lived and worked.

At the time of his death, Lex was announcing pregame and halftime shows for the San Francisco 49ers football team, as well as maintaining a continued interest in the Hunger Outreach program in Fresno. In the *ProRodeo Sports News* article, his daughter said that her dad and Shirley "for all practical purposes . . . started public television in Fresno when they took over, developed, and ran Channel 18," KVPT Valley Public Television.

He always knew how he wanted to be remembered, said his daughter: "A very simple service and a good stiff drink for his friends."

"Lex never liked to blow his own horn," said then PRCA executive vice president Bob Eidson. "Probably by choice, he never got the recognition he deserved pertaining to the growth of the rodeo business. Or in life, for that matter."

Lex Connelly was inducted into the ProRodeo Hall of Fame in 1985.

Louise was home on the X9 Ranch when she heard the news. The love of her life was gone. Heartbroken and beyond consolation, she aimlessly walked around the house and out into the soft spring air. She had recently added a negative-edge swimming pool on her property, and as she stood there wondering what else life was going to throw at her, a white dove appeared. (Actually it was a white pigeon, but Louise always thought of it as a dove.) It flew across the water and landed on the other side of the pool. Immediately Louise knew that Lex was letting her know he was all right, and that she too would be all right— eventually.

From then on the anniversary of Lex's death appeared on every one of Louise's appointment calendars.

Three days later she was taking pictures at a rodeo in Cave Creek, then on to the Globe competition. She went to New York in May, a trip she took almost every year to visit her father and stepmother (Joseph Larocque had married Edna Strongfeld Callaway on August 7, 1936.). Her busy scheduled continued to keep her occupied, but her thoughts of Lex never ceased. Reflecting on those rare occasions when they had met up with each other on the rodeo circuit, Louise may have wondered what she could look forward to in the coming years.

She must have decided travel was the remedy for her grief, for she headed to Israel and Italy that summer, returning in time

Robbie Christie on Lollipop, 1984, Globe, Arizona
COURTESY OF SERPA PHOTOGRAPHY, L.L.C.

to photograph the Turquoise Circuit Finals in Farmington, New Mexico, that November.

Since many cowboys cannot compete on a national level for a variety of reasons, the Professional Rodeo Cowboys Association divided the country into twelve rodeo circuits. The Turquoise Circuit consists of twenty rodeos held each year in Arizona and New Mexico, thereby keeping "weekend cowboys" closer to home.

Every fall the Turquoise Circuit sends its top twelve contestants, two in each event, to the finals rodeo, which is held in various towns across Arizona and New Mexico. Louise photographed many of these rodeos throughout the years as well as the final competitions.

"I remember when there used to be only one rodeo on a circuit," she told the *Arizona Daily Star* in 1984. "There was a time when you knew everybody on it. Now there are five to six rodeos going on every weekend. There are over 600 rodeos in a year."

"I've photographed children in junior rodeos who are now competing as full-grown men," she said, and she was also taking pictures of the children of those first cowboys she had encountered almost thirty years prior.

As the number of rodeos grew, so did the list of accidents and deaths. Louise was not immune from witnessing many of these tragedies.

In Yuma a bulldogger was killed right in front of her when he jumped off his horse and onto a steer, only to have his foot catch in his horse's stirrup. The horse peeled off and pulled the man from the steer, right under the horse's hooves.

"It's horrifying to see the horse dragging the rider, right there, and not to be able to do anything about it," she said. "He was dead before he got to the end of the arena, because he went right under the horse, and the horse just pummeled him to death in a panic.

"I kept thinking there must be something I could do. But if I tried to lunge for the horse and grab the reins it would have thrown him more over the guy. I've seen a lot of people hurt. That was the most severe. You hate to see people hurt and you hate to see animals hurt and that happens every once in a while."

She used to involve herself in these accidents but quickly learned the cowboys preferred her behind the camera to shoot whatever calamity befell them. "Many times I saw friends getting hurt," she told an *Arizona Daily Star* reporter in 1984. "I used to drop my camera and start to cry because I was worrying about them. When I'd visit them in the hospital the first thing they'd ask is, 'Did you get the picture?' I had to learn to stand my ground and do my job. My job is to capture that moment. The cowboys could care less how I feel inside at the time. They want the action down on film."

She also saw many of them pray before climbing into the arena. "It's a very religious bunch," she said in a 1994 *Houston Chronicle* article. "Many of the guys pump themselves up somehow before they go on; they either hyperventilate, slap themselves on the cheeks hard—and I mean really hard—or do jumping exercises. It's to [get] the surge of adrenaline going. It does strengthen you."

Back in Tucson, Sanders Galleries held a very successful exhibition of Louise's work, and she won first place in the 1984 International Photography Hall of Fame and Museum's Second National Finals Pro-Rodeo Photography Contest. She had placed second the prior year.

Louise, however, decided to try her hand at a new venture—writing.

"Hagar the Hero" is the true story of a Hungarian komondor guard dog that plies his talents at a sheep station located on the slopes of Colorado's Pikes Peak. Louise became fascinated with this large, grayish-white, shaggy-haired, lumbering canine that protects sheep with no thought for its own safety. Her story about Hagar and his narrow escape from the jaws of a hungry coyote appeared in the December 1984 issue of *Owl* magazine, a publication out of Toronto, Canada, that has been broadening the curiosities of children since 1976.

Three years later, *Owl* published another of her stories, "Growing Up: A Taos Pueblo Indian Story," told from the perspective of a teenage girl who likes rock music and the latest fashions, but who also immerses herself in her own culture in a little village outside of Taos, New Mexico. The young girl relates the differences she encounters between the two cultures and how she manages to live in and respect the principles of both.

Correspondence from *Owl* editors to Louise expressed their appreciation for her submissions, saying they had been well received. She also wrote several articles about rodeoing, but the two children's stories seem to be all she authored in the juvenile genre.

About a year after Lex's death, Louise began spending a considerable amount of time in Santa Fe, New Mexico. She had reconnected with an old friend from her New York school days, John Burchenal "Burch" Ault, who had served for fifteen years as provost of the two campuses of St. John's College, one located in Annapolis, Maryland, and the other in the secluded foothills of the Sangre de Cristo Mountains on the eastern edge of Santa Fe. He was an attractive Yale man with impeccable manners and a penchant for poetry. (Louise's daughter Lauren says he reminded her of actor Jimmy Stewart.) His wife of over thirty-five years had died shortly before he and Louise reunited.

The relationship between Louise and Burch quickly developed into a whirlwind romance. Her lengthy stint as a single woman since divorcing Tex Serpa over twenty-five years prior, plus the recent death of Lex Connelly, may have had some influence on her decision to marry again. Both she and Burch were suffering from the loss of a loved one, and this might have been all the impetus needed to push two old friends into a loving liaison.

Louise and Burch were married October 12, 1985, at Tucson's celebrated Arizona Inn. The evening before the ceremony, her dear friends Jack and Aline Goodman threw the couple a party that lasted long into the night.

The following day Louise donned a cobalt-blue dress adorned with a two-strand pearl necklace and made her way to the inn for the ceremony. As she stood with Burch to take her vows, she suddenly realized she could not get her engagement ring off her finger so Burch could put on her wedding ring. Apparently all that tequila the night before had made her fingers swell. She fidgeted and fussed, but the ring refused to budge. The ceremony continued, but all of Louise's entertaining antics as she tried to remove the ring were caught on the wedding video.

The celebration at the Arizona Inn continued until midnight, when breakfast was served to all who remained. The couple honeymooned by traveling to Santa Fe, then on to New York to have their union blessed by both families. Their final stop was Annapolis, Maryland, probably to visit the St. John's campus there. They settled in Santa Fe at Burch's home, although Louise never once thought of giving up her house on the X9 Ranch. And she certainly had no intention of missing any Tucson Rodeo, or any other rodeo, for that matter, even though Burch rarely accompanied her on her photographic assignments.

She traveled the Turquoise Circuit through Arizona and New Mexico that fall and photographed the finals in Phoenix before heading back to Australia to visit Sydney, Dubbo, and the island of Tasmania.

She returned to England in February of 1986, and again in October of the same year, visiting Scotland as well. In between she flew off to Virginia to photograph the Keswick Horse Show, which has been around since the early 1900s. She continued to shoot this event over the ensuing years.

She divided her time among living with Burch in Santa Fe, touring the world, keeping up her demanding schedule, and staying at the X9 Ranch.

According to her half sister Anne, Louise hoped Burch would travel with her, go to all the interesting places she planned to see. She envisioned having a fascinating life with him.

Louise and Burch Ault
COURTESY OF SERPA FAMILY

Burch preferred to stay home, however, and wanted Louise to adjust her lifestyle to his more sedate regime. He was looking for a dutiful wife to entertain his friends and maintain the home, just as his first wife had done for so many years. Louise did her best to adapt. Anne recalls that her half sister "really tried hard to do what wives of her generation were trained to do," but it was not in her disposition to be the submissive spouse. "I need to get up and make Burch breakfast," she would announce, but what she really wanted to do was head out into the desert and take pictures of the sunrise, the flowering cactus, and majestic mountains, not be stuck behind a frying pan and washing dishes three times a day.

The couple truly loved each other, but their modes of living were so different that it was difficult for them to bond. For seven years they struggled to make the marriage work.

Chapter 16

It never occurred to me that I was anything more than a good recorder of whatever I was shooting.

Burch Ault was an avid fundraiser for a variety of programs and events from New Mexico to New York, chairing many of the sponsoring organizations. On one of these occasions, Louise found herself face-to-face with George H. W. Bush just a few years before he became the forty-first president of the United States. What they discussed during that evening's dinner in Bush's honor is not known, but Louise had her trusty glass of tequila in hand when a photographer snapped the twosome, which may have kept the conversation more than a little lively.

In demand at art events and social gatherings, she had to weigh the allure of these occasions against Burch's desire to have her home in Santa Fe with him. All too often she was forced to make difficult decisions about where she should spend her time. Regardless of the strain it may have caused in her marriage, she never considered missing the annual February gathering of Tucson's La Fiesta de los Vaqueros.

At the 1988 rodeo former Tucson mayor Lew C. Murphy stopped the festival in midperformance, brought Louise out to the center of the arena, and presented her with two dozen dew-dripping red roses and a large copper letter, dedicating the entire day to her photographic endeavors on behalf of the Tucson Rodeo. Louise was flabbergasted.

"It never occurred to me that I was anything more than a good recorder of whatever I was shooting," she told the Rodeo Historical Society, amazed anyone paid that much attention to a sixty-two-year-old, somewhat gray-haired woman who still maneuvered around the arena as if she were an energetic, enthusiastic young athlete. She told an *Arizona Daily Star* reporter in 1984, "I'll never quit. I've never reached my peak. I'm always working over my head." And in *Rodeo*, she said:

> *The adrenaline rush that you get the minute you walk into an arena is phenomenal, anyway—it's wonderful. I always feel ten years younger when I get out of an arena than I do when I go in, no matter how tired I am when I start.*
>
> *There's always excitement. Getting a terrific piece of action on film is exciting. Often you never know what is on the film until you get the proof sheet. Sometimes you get things you didn't know you ever had. I never get over the excitement of looking at a proof sheet and getting a photograph that's simply marvelous.*

The following year she shot one of her most famous pictures at the Tucson Rodeo. *Cotton Eye* depicts a horse that has unceremoniously dumped its rider. With all its legs in midair, the animal looks as though it is about to land all four of its powerful hooves on the poor, defenseless cowboy. The picture clearly demonstrates the dangers many a fallen cowboy experiences.

Because she now spent more of her time in Santa Fe, Louise found venues nearby in which to exhibit her work. In 1987 she had a showing of her photographs in the little town of Galisteo,

Cotton Eye, *1989, ProRodeo Cowboys Association, Tucson, Arizona*
COURTESY OF SERPA PHOTOGRAPHY, L.L.C.

just south of Santa Fe, and she was featured at Santa Fe's Rutgers Barclay Gallery in 1989. In this exhibit another of her celebrated pictures, *Hud*, taken in 1971, was used on the publicity poster advertising the event.

Cowboy Jim Mihalek was riding Hud the day she shot the picture. Hud seemed extra ornery as he left the chute, and in Louise's photograph the horse is leaping straight into the air, back arched, head and tail aimed toward the ground. Jim is in the opposite position, his bottom still attached to the horse but his legs, arms, and head curved upward toward the heavens as he holds on with all his strength and determination.

Louise remembered this as one of the first sequences she ever shot:

I didn't have a motor-drive on the camera in those days, but with the hand-held camera, I could do five pictures in an eight-second ride without too much blurring from advancing the shutter manually.

Jim rode that horse; he didn't get thrown. The sad and ironic thing is that he failed to mark the horse out of the chute—he didn't have his feet up. He had a fantastic ride, which everybody knows, but he didn't get a marking on it because of that rule infraction.

These pictures show how athletic both the man and the beast have to be to survive in action like this.

On November 26, 1988, Joseph Larocque died in New York just a month shy of his eighty-seventh birthday. Louise had been with her father the week before he passed away, knowing his time was limited. She missed him terribly, so she did what always took her mind off troubles—she hiked up her Levi's, put on a sparkling silver belt buckle, donned her broad-brimmed hat to keep the sun out of her eyes, and headed out the door, cameras in hand.

She was driving a Saab at the time, putting over thirty-five thousand miles a year on the petite but sturdy automobile sporting the personalized license plate "PHOTOG." The back bumper held a sticker from the Santa Fe Rodeo and one for Tucson's hometown western radio station, KiiM 99.5.

The coupe was filled to the brim with photo equipment, hats, boots, and a couple changes of clothing. Stashed somewhere underneath all this paraphernalia was probably a delicious, robust bottle of Jose Cuervo Gold.

Her rodeo gamut included a stopover in the prison town of Florence, Arizona. "There used to be prison rodeos,"

Hud, *1971, ProRodeo Cowboys Association, Tucson, Arizona*
Courtesy of Serpa Photography, L.L.C.

Louise at the Little Bear Ranch, 1992, McLeod, Montana
© Bruce Weber

Louise later recalled. "They didn't have roping stock in the state penitentiary, but they imported rough stock. It was a significant leveler for them too: big cell-block bullies—who in normal prison-life would just beat up on the smaller men—would get out there full of bravado, and as often as not, they would get flattened during the first two jumps."

She singled out one particular cowboy who seemed to end up periodically in the Florence State Prison. Glen Adair never did anything too terrible, but he often found himself on the wrong side of the slammer for a short while. Wanting to stay in touch with his rodeo buddies who would come to Florence to participate in the Junior Parada every Thanksgiving weekend, Glen volunteered to play in the Stars Behind Bars band, which, according to Louise, consisted of "totally tone-deaf guys that

Glen Adair, 1964, Arizona Rodeo Association, Sonoita, Arizona
Courtesy of Serpa Photography, L.L.C.

get into the band on purpose so they can be let out to come play at the rodeo on that weekend. And Glen somehow always managed to get into Stars Behind Bars, so he could come say hi."

Glen probably would not make the grade in today's rodeo, as Louise tendered the participants were in much better shape than when she first started shooting in the arena. When she wrote about Glen in her book *Rodeo*, which was published in 1994, she noted, "Today's rodeo is very much a competition of real athletes. They don't have nearly as much fun as we used to have! They're in training all the time. They don't go out drinking, smoking, partying, and misbehaving—they don't have the time. They keep better hours, and they have to keep in top physical shape."

"There is an image that the guys are supposed to have: long sleeves with a hat, properly clean. It's like any sports uniform. You can't compete in the arena in a T-shirt or baseball cap. There will be a short sleeve or two in there," she said, "but that's a no-no in the arena."

She admitted she finally had to learn how to shoot color photography because the cowboys wanted it. But she refused to learn how to process color, claiming there was not as much play in the feel of the photograph. She had more poetic license in developing black-and-white prints in which she could play with light and darkness, leaving more to the imagination.

"To me, the rodeo has always been black and white, though many of the things I do now have to be shot in color. Frankly," she told a *Tucson Lifestyle* reporter in 1993, "I've never liked color as well. It doesn't have the impact or the pathos. Maybe color is too immediate. In color photography, there is little latitude for your own personal expression. Black-and-white has more impact, more feeling; it has more wrinkles."

As she made her way from one rodeo town to another, Louise began to realize she had to make a decision about her floundering marriage.

Burch Ault was no match for the energies Louise exerted. She "was such a force of nature," half sister Anne says, "that she needed someone who could keep up with her personality and her drive and energy level, and he was a patrician East Coast, blue-blooded, Republican type, and it was just a bad thing. It certainly wasn't a good fit temperamentally."

None of Louise's husbands was a bad man, according to Anne. Louise, however, was so strongly directed and independent that it was hard for her to find someone who could handle her dynamic disposition.

At the end of the year she left Burch and returned to the X9 Ranch to figure out what she wanted to do.

Chapter 17

The leopard's head alone was visible—enormous with blazing eyes in the spotlights.

While Louise was still regrouping after her separation from Burch Ault and living at her house on the X9 Ranch, she left home one evening in a downpour to attend an opening at the Etherton Gallery, located in Tucson's historic Odd Fellows Hall. The gallery, known as "one of Tucson's early and most enduring contemporary art spaces," has been a Tucson mainstay since 1981 with extensive exhibits of vintage, classic, and contemporary photography. Louise donned a long yellow duster and broad-brimmed western hat to keep off the rain, looking every bit a cowgirl coming in from the range after wrangling cattle all day.

As soon as she stepped through the gallery doors, owner Terry Etherton knew who she was because, according to gallery director Hannah Glasston, her "personality preceded her often."

"She was ultra-gracious," that night, recalls Hannah, and "said wonderful things about his [Terry's] photography gallery." Terry offered to have a showing of Louise's work at the

Temple Gallery, which Terry managed for over twenty years, located in an upstairs arcade at Tucson's Temple of Music and Art. He had no trouble selling her unique prints and continued to display her work in at least two more well-received solo exhibits at the Temple Gallery.

The hat Louise wore that evening may have been damaged by the rain, but if she was wearing one of her favorite Resistol toppers (the name means they resist all weather), it might have survived the downpour. She claimed to wear the same hat for twenty-five years, and it certainly took a beating during rodeos when she often threw it into the air to get a horse's attention, causing the horse to perk up its ears so she could get a better picture. This was, of course, outside the rodeo arena.

While working the 4H finals at the Phoenix fairgrounds one year, she wandered over to an area where crews were setting up Indian exhibits. In one of the booths, shoved into the back of a bottom shelf, she saw a rolled-up, wizened black hatband and quickly realized true silver conchos adorned the timeworn ribbon. The seller wanted $40 for the dusty piece of fabric, but Louise carried very little cash and he refused to take her check. No sooner did she turn to head back toward the arena to find someone who might lend her the money than a man walked up to the booth expressing an interest in the dilapidated hatband. Fortunately he did not have cash either, and the footrace was on to see who could get back to the booth first with cash in hand. She liked to boast she beat him by a mere ten feet, and that coveted remnant adorned every hat she owned from then on.

In 1990 Louise and several of her pals headed for Africa to visit old friends. Of course she carted along several cameras, and shot some of her best photographs of African flora and fauna. She kept a journal on this trip, starting with the flight out of Los Angeles to London on June 12, which she noted was delayed for more than eight hours.

Two days later the entourage landed in Nairobi. Edward, their driver on this leg of the trip, kept the group on trail and on time.

"Saw my first flame trees and the tipu tree [Pride of Bolivia] with yellow flowers," Louise wrote on the first day of their adventure. "We all fell into showers, short naps and came down for dinner. I had a martini before [dinner] with not one but *two* marascino [*sic*] cherries in it can you believe. Dinner at the Tamarind Restaurant [in Nairobi] with the best soup and as unbelievable, sweet crab, so sweet & good it was a shame to use butter."

The next day as they set off on tour, Edward educated the group by describing the three main tribes in Kenya—the Kikuyu, Luo, and Luhya—then headed to a giraffe center for a lecture on these stoic, stately mammals. "After lunch at Horseman's in Karen" [a neighborhood in Nairobi], Louise wrote, "we had our first animal drive in the Nairobi Natl. Park—herds of hartebeest, impala, olive baboon, cape buffalo and best of all, a herd of giraffe which should be among my best shots."

Edward left them as they flew off to the city of Arusha. The eighty-mile drive from Arusha to Ngorogora left Louise in awe:

Arusha to Ngorogora through fields of coffee; tea, banana trees; cassava planted between bananas which is the staple diet during hard time—boiled or ground as porridge; croton trees, Euphorbia trees; yellow backed acacia. Baobab tree on way up out of Rift Valley. Top of hill & dark we were met by a very cross female elephant and had to wait an unscheduled ½ hour till she decided to move. Crater Lodge was decidedly primitive. No hot water, johns didn't flush, rooms cold. The Lodge itself is nice—fireplaces & beautiful view of the rim.

She spent several days in the area before heading to Lake Manyara National Park at the base of Rift Valley, where she spotted acacias, wild figs, wild mangos, blue monkeys, black-and-white long-tailed fiscal shrikes, white-backed pelicans, black-and-white ground hornbills, giraffes with ox peckers on their backs, and wildebeests with calves. Her cameras almost smoked she shot so many pictures.

At night she wrote about listening to lions roar, and she reported that "the Egyptian geese near our room woke us at dawn."

As she departed for the next stop, Louise noted in her journal, "I miss my man—wish he was here to see all this!" Burch Ault was still very much part of her life.

The group cleared immigration and customs in Nairobi, with Louise mentioning she had spent $9,000 on "three zebra carpets, one zebra hide, two purses & various sundries."

She found her accommodations at the one-hundred-acre Mt. Kenya Safari Club "terribly chic. The drive up—lovely, tho my neck was disaster . . . which resulted in my arriving in tears, more of frayed tension nerves than pain." Yet once she saw her room she apparently forgot her discomfort. She had a "sitting room with fireplace, a welcome cake, letter with a single rose. The fire gets lit each evening at 6:00 by which time it's raining and cold. We dress for dinner with drinks in the bar first. The food is fabulous. Mt. Kenya appeared and disappeared in clouds."

She was enamored with more than the scenery. "The shopping was best yet—popped for our 3 giraffe carving which is being shipped along with leather pillows. Bought 2 necklaces—one a tribal one, the other a big mersham bead & silver that I may have to keep; 3 dresses—Marty, Aline & Johanna; a bracelet for Anne; necklace for Edna [all friends and relatives back in the States]; elephant cupboard handles, and a duffle to haul it all in."

After checking out of the Mt. Kenya Safari Club, the ensemble visited an animal orphanage with "elands & babies; colobus monkeys with beautiful white furry tails, dik-diks [small antelope], and best of all—bongos [large antelope], free in a large wooded enclosure. The guard chummed them up for me—should be good shots."

"We stopped at the site of the old burned down Silverbeck Hotel situated exactly on the equator, to have a water demonstration," then "on to the Aberdare Country Club for a delicious lunch in incredible surroundings. Bougainvillea, enormous euphorbia candelabra, cassia. After lunch, we loaded into big busses to the Ark which was a whole different experience."

The Ark is an expansive edifice located smack in the middle of Aberdare National Park. It resembles a gigantic Noah's Ark in which tourists can safely view some of Kenya's most exotic animals and birds, dine on scrumptious fare, and be awakened in the middle of the night if a particularly interesting animal comes to graze at the waterhole or partake of the salt lick.

> [It's] *like being on a ship. It was a hushed and quiet time; drizzling, foggy, clearing from time to time to shoot Bush buck, cape buffalo, numerous birds, Egyptian geese, red knobbed coot, slender billed weavers and 3 "white" rhinos. The largest visible one stayed way back in the trees with her new baby. Gazelle in and out but 3 male capes never far away.*
>
> *4:30 a.m., the buzzer sounded 3 times, the warning for a leopard. . . . The leopard's head alone was visible—enormous with blazing eyes in the spotlights. The gazelles stamped and barked & fled over the hill. The leopard got up and lazily came past the Ark, huge, well fed. We went back to bed till dawn. A single large male elephant was outside who did not like the sound of my motor drive.*

Boarding the tour car the next day, the assembly stopped at Lake Nakuou.

"The lake was swarming: water buck, red buck, fleets of wart hogs & babies, pelicans, marabou stork which can kill a flamingo, a tawny eagle eating plover eggs out of the nest, and a shot of the single remaining egg."

Still in the Rift Valley, Louise and the others spent the night in the Lake Naivasha Hotel surrounded by "trimmed up flat-topped acacias with multitudes of birds—our first parrots. Good food, good sleep under mosquito netting."

According to Louise, "Naivasha is a bird watcher's heaven. Fish eagles, hornbills, osprey, egrets, red-knobbed coots, black cranes. Wish we had more time to absorb & explore. A beautiful place to return to.

"On the road to Nairobi we started seeing wonderful big, well-made heavy baskets. We stopped naturally & there was a man in a Bud Lite shirt from whom I bought [stepmother] Edna's fawn colored seed necklace."

Louise spent the evening with friends in Karen, Kenya, and then lunched at the Carnivore Restaurant (which, according to its advertisement, serves "ostrich, crocodile and camel, that is roasted over charcoal and carved at your table") "before boarding the plane in Nairobi for Kenya's Maasai Mara National Reserve."

Easy flight, and we were met out on the plain [Serengeti] by a driver from Little Governors Camp. We had double tents with private loos—tents behind with tiled floors & showers and bidets. The water was heated by a fire outside. No electricity but good Coleman lamps. Main tent had table, two good beds, a place to hang clothes. We were told to zip flaps when leaving—not for mosquitoes but animals. Baboons, etc. often in. Hippos are in the swampy pond just in front of the tent and elephants come down to drink in the night, so there is a guard who patrols.

I started off our evening well by trying to show Squeak how her bidet worked [Squeakee Wangenstein, a friend of Louise's]. Leaning over the "beast" I tried to get it to spray and while examining it at close range it finally busted loose— shooting me right in the face! I laughed so hard I lost my footing and fell backwards into the shower.

Saw our first lilac breasted roller & sooty chat [African songbirds].

Her journal ends abruptly after this last entry, although she mentions on her calendar that she was planning on taking a balloon safari while in Nairobi. Her descriptions of the birds and beasts, the countryside and the people, are more than enough to surmise that Louise thoroughly relished and absorbed everything there was to see on this three-week African expedition.

Two weeks later, she headed for Winthrop, Washington, to attend Mia's wedding to James Kuhns on July 28. The marriage lasted about four years; Mia eventually returned to live in Tucson.

In between returning home from Africa and leaving for Winthrop, Louise managed to squeeze in the Santa Fe Rodeo and probably a long-overdue visit with her husband.

Later that summer, she moved into a second house on the X9 Ranch property and started renovating it. She loved the lower acreage of the ranch property and decided she needed a project to keep her occupied as she sorted out her troubled marriage.

Chapter 18

You can make or break a picture in the printing.

Rodeos kept Louise busy after her sojourn to Africa, although medical issues impeded her somewhat. She had a hernia operation in 1990 followed by cataract surgery in 1991. In April of that year, she was back in the hospital recovering from hand surgery. That bull she had hit on the road to Vail a few years back caused her to severely jam her thumbs against the steering wheel of the car. When the pain reached the level of intolerance, she had her thumbs fused at the lower joints so she could keep shooting.

Even with her busy schedule she regretted not taking more photography classes. "There were so many times that I was supposed to be doing a job and I didn't know how to do it or I was sure it was not going to turn out well," she remembered in the 2004 Rodeo Historical Society interview. "I did not know anything about light meters," devices that read how bright or dark the light is in order to adjust the film's exposure.

"It didn't make a difference to me in the arena because I could get an overall reading, but I was shooting into shadows and then turned around and shot right into sun." Film cameras make it more difficult to go from one extreme exposure to another because the exposure change has to be made manually. With the quick action in a rodeo arena, it was practically impossible to make this sudden change. She lamented:

> *Nobody ever told me what to do there. I just figured out by looking at negatives that I had ruined that I was mis-shooting, that I was going to get in the arena with black and white [film] and open up the camera to a 5 or 6 [F-stop] and shoot it at a 500 or 1000 depending what Tri-X [Kodak film] was in those days. And then I would under-develop and that seemed to even it out. And I was inadvertently doing what is now called, with great mystique, the "zone system," which I didn't have a clue what they were talking about, which was to shoot for the shadows basically.*
>
> *Digital is going to change everything—it has already. I still like the feeling, the tactile feeling of the film, versus something that is digital. You can change anything you want but I don't think there is the depth in digital photography that you still get with film.*

And while she was often quoted as saying, "You can make or break a picture in the printing," Louise also believed, as she said in a 1995 Tucson television interview, that "the reason some of the rodeo pictures are more exciting in the past than they are today is because of the length of the lens. Photographers now will sit way back on the other side of the ring against the fence and use a 300 or 400 mm lens, 500 even," whereas Louise felt she could incorporate more of the arena around the rider and horse instead of isolating them, which is what a long lens will do to the subject.

"It foreshortens the action. It brings the background right up against the horse that's bucking. I didn't have those long

Louise hanging on the fence, circa 1970s

COURTESY OF SERPA FAMILY

lenses. Number one, I couldn't afford them and number two, I could not see rodeo from that distance. I wanted to be right on top of it. So I used a 90 or 105 [mm lens], depending on what camera I was using at the time."

She applied all of her photographic abilities not only at rodeos and cutting shows but also on her international treks to Africa and Australia. With her detailed pictures of wildlife and native plants starting to receive as much acclaim as her rodeo prints, she was back in Australia in the fall of 1991, stopping by the Great Barrier Reef, as well as taking a sojourn to New Zealand.

Yet no matter where she was in the world, she always made it back to be in the arena every February to shoot the Tucson Rodeo.

Eighteen-year-old bull rider Gary Williams met Louise at the Tucson Rodeo in 1967. Over the years, Gary made his way from the floor of the arena to the front offices, becoming Tucson Rodeo general manager in 1994.

He is the first person to admit that Louise did "more to promote Tucson Rodeo than anyone in its history. The way she captured images was unlike anything that had been done previously. She brought the sport of rodeo in a very, very vivid way to people who had never seen rodeo. She really is a gem." And, according to Gary, "She had no fear."

He also loved Louise's sense of humor. One particular January, both he and Louise were present at the Turquoise Circuit finals, which were being held out near the Old Tucson movie grounds. Gary remembers that for some reason, "They put all the security people in cavalry uniforms.

"They used to be pretty lax about people bringing in beer because everyone would party behind the arena and everyone had an ice chest. But then they started cracking down. This day was particularly, unseasonably hot and dusty. As soon as the rodeo was over everyone was ready for a beer."

Louise had worn a sweater most of the day, as morning temperatures were still quite cool, but by midday she was uncomfortably hot.

"Someone hands her a beer," recalls Gary, "which she was eternally thankful for. A security guy walks up to her in one of those cavalry outfits and tells her she cannot drink the beer, that she has to pour it out. She said, 'I will absolutely not pour this beer out. The only place this beer is going is down my throat.'"

Feeling somewhat intimidated at confronting a gray-haired woman in her mid-sixties, the guard called for more security. Five or six more men showed up and surrounded Louise.

By this time several cowboys, their curiosity piqued, made their way toward Louise to see what the ruckus was all about, Gary among them. They asked Louise if there was a problem, and she matter-of-factly replied, "They're trying to take my beer." Well, Gary and the other cowboys were not about to let that happen. Gary said, "No, they're not going to take your beer," and Louise agreed. "I know they're not, that's what I'm trying to tell them."

Throughout this confrontation Louise continued to drink her beer. Word began to spread that someone was harassing Louise, and before long about thirty cowboys were standing around telling the cavalry to back off. But security would have none of it and insisted Louise pour out her beer. Louise, however, refused to listen and continued to consume her brew.

One of the cowboys piped up, "None of you is big enough or man enough to make her pour that beer out," and things turned toward ugly. Names were called and more security arrived. Someone called the sheriff for backup.

"Finally," Gary remembers, "Louise finishes her beer and tells security, 'You may now have the can.'" She handed the empty container to one of the guards, pushed her way through the crowd, and headed for her car. Nobody messed with Louise.

The next day she brought her own cooler of refreshments to the arena. The cowboys joked they had saved her hide, but Louise would have none of it. "I don't need any saving—you all know that."

"And she was right," confirms Gary.

Chapter 19

I tried to retire a couple of times.
It didn't work.

Aches and pains are part of growing older, and because of her active lifestyle, Louise began experiencing some of the symptoms that come with a vigorous and demanding profession. Her knees gave her a lot of trouble—all that stooping for the best shot and scooting under fences to stay out of the way of bucking broncs started catching up with her. Through the years, along with being stomped by a bull and slammed between a fence and gate by an outraged horse, she had been kicked in the back of the neck by a bareback horse, roped around the neck by a wayward lasso, and knocked over by a steer wrestler. Two back operations left her a little slow to get up in the morning, and her evening shots of tequila were sometimes all that relieved her tired muscles. Yet she never considered slowing down, and she certainly had no intention of leaving the rodeo arena. In her 1994 interview with *Tucson Guide Quarterly*, Louise reiterated her feelings about retiring that she had expressed ten years earlier:

I tried to retire a couple of times. It didn't work. I'm fundamentally incapable of just going to a rodeo and watching it.

Louise at the Tucson Rodeo, circa 1998

COURTESY OF SHARI VAN ALSBURG

*It's the whole feel in the air. If I go to shoot and am tired when
I start, I always get a shot of adrenaline. It's the greatest in
the world, and I come out feeling 20 years younger than when
I went in.*

*It [photography] is a wonderful, wonderful tool to life. It
sharpens everything you do, everything you see. You never
know where you are going to end up. I've worked my way
around the world with it and I've had fun every minute of the
time I have been doing it. You can't ask for much more than
that.*

She refused to allow her physical ills to prevent her from
traveling, and even though both of her parents had passed
away, as well as her stepfather, Gilbert Goodwin Browne, she
continued to make her annual trek to New York, mainly to visit
her stepmother, Edna. While in the city she often met with Bruce
Weber, their friendship lasting throughout Louise's lifetime. She
visited his ranch in Montana every year and the two of them,
along with a handful of other artists and photographers, exhibited their work at one of the galleries in the area.

Now considered an authority on action photography, she
was frequently asked her opinion about shooting specific activities, particularly sporting events. In an undated letter to Jim
Dickinson, then education curator of the Hubbard Museum
of the American West (the Museum of the Horse) in Ruidoso
Downs, New Mexico, she gave him her view on "shooting from
the hip":

*"Shooting from the hip" to record the optimum moment of
motion or light is a challenge. It pays to understand whatever
sport or activity is involved as anticipation is an essential element in action photography. That and being constantly aware
of what goes on around you—be it an expression on a face, a*

sudden change of light or the peak of action. It means being ready for the expected as well as the spontaneous. It means reflexive shooting. The rewards are frequently fascinating and, to me, totally addictive.

In August 1992 the *New Yorker* published a short piece about Louise's work. The author of the article, Ingrid Seshi, whom Louise had met in Montana at Bruce Weber's ranch, frankly admitted she "knew nothing and cared nothing about rodeo photography" until she met Louise. Comparing her work to that of nineteenth-century English photographer Eadweard James Muybridge, who pioneered photographic studies in motion and became famous for his large, powerful Yosemite Valley, California, photographs, Seshi claimed,

Serpa has also revolutionized thinking about bodies in motion. . . . It's hard to believe your eyes when you first see how wild in form her pictures are—both the horses and the cowboys take on shapes so free from gravity that if you didn't know better you'd think they were made of rubber, or were the products of trick photography. . . . Her rodeo photographs are the result of all her knowledge of her subject, and embody her deep respect for both the animal and the human participants.

We went through the pile of pictures she had with her over and over again. And her talk—about life, her work, and the way rodeo has changed—held us rapt. It was a whole philosophy of life that we heard, expressed in such advice as "Never don't pay attention."

Around this time the Tucson Airport Authority put on a one-artist show of Louise's work, allowing visitors from all around the globe to view her death-defying photographs as they traveled to and from the Old Pueblo.

For several years she had been shooting rodeos in small Mexican towns just across the US border and, according to rodeo manager Gary Williams, she gained the respect and friendship of Juan Nuñez, the liaison between the Pima County Sheriff's Department and various police agencies in Sonora, Mexico. Juan was also an avid rodeo fan, and when he attended the Tucson Rodeo, he usually brought several visiting dignitaries with him.

According to Gary, Juan's wife's family owned a large ranch in the little town of Bacadéhuachi in southern Sonora where they homebrewed a tasty concoction called Bacanora—basically moonshine tequila. Juan always had a jug with him when he arrived in Tucson. Once the rodeo was over, the jug was passed around a small, elite group of friends. No need for anything fancy such as sipping from a glass, just a swig out of the bottle before passing the flask on to the next partaker. Of course, no one had any idea what proof this potion was, and it probably did not matter to anyone sampling the beverage.

Eventually Louise was included in this after-rodeo party, particularly since her penchant for tequila was well known around the rodeo circuit. The first time she grabbed the jug and took a large swig of Bacanora, she swilled it around in her mouth, and then took another big mouthful. She looked thoughtful, Gary recalls, and finally she said, "You know, once you get past the inner tube taste, it's not bad stuff." She became part of the group immediately and remained fast friends with Nuñez.

By the fall of 1992 Louise knew her marriage to Burch Ault was over. She loved him dearly, as well as his family. He had five children with his first wife and they had accepted Louise into their domestic fold, but Burch and Louise had lived in two different worlds for too long—both found it difficult to change their ways at this stage in their lives. The divorce was final on December 30, 1992.

Burch had previously sold his house in Santa Fe and was liv-ing with Louise at her home on the X9 Ranch. With the divorce pending, he left Arizona at the beginning of December and returned to New Mexico, where he remained the rest of his life, continuing his lifelong involvement in education. He remarried in 1994 and died in Santa Fe on October 29, 2008, at the age of eighty-two.

Three unsuccessful marriages must have left Louise feeling very alone, particularly since her one true love, Lex Connelly, was not around to pick up the pieces after this last failed union. As her half sister Anne once said, "It's possible that the one that gets away is the only one you can live with."

Chapter 20

I'll always do Tucson.

"You shoot when it's cold, when it's rainy, when it's windy, when it's hot," Louise reported in her 1995 television interview. "It doesn't make any difference, rodeos don't stop."

On February 24, 1993, around two o'clock in the afternoon, right at the height of the Tucson Rodeo, a blinding rainstorm blew across the arena, challenging drenched and dripping cowboys as they maneuvered bucking horses against equally challenging winds, fighting for a decent ride time on spooked mounts. Those riders still slated to perform would be at a definite disadvantage as thunder crashed and rumbled across the blackening sky.

Louise slogged through the mud trying to get the best possible shots in this driving deluge, but she was on unsure ground as she fought for footage in the soggy stadium. She landed on the ground before she could catch herself, reinjuring an already battered and damaged knee.

She made it to the rodeo dinner and dance two days later, but within the month she was in the hospital, recuperating from knee surgery.

"I was a pretty good athlete," she said a year later while writing her book *Rodeo*, "and my reflexes aren't bad. Also, I didn't realize how much body English I put into shooting, getting down or getting in the right position or being able to move fast, until last winter when I couldn't with my bad knee. It drove me bonkers. I couldn't get down or kneel to do certain things. I've since had the knee 'scoped,' and it's doing fine."

Shortly after returning from shooting the Prescott Rodeo that July, however, she fell down a flight of stairs, again injuring her knee. Despite the pain she never considered withdrawing from a rodeo or canceling an already scheduled trip. She put together an exhibition of her work for the Museum of the Southwest in Midland, Texas, before heading to Montana that August for her annual holiday on Bruce Weber's spread and to participate in an exhibit at the Danforth Gallery in Livingston. She made it to the Sonoita rodeo that September, leaving almost immediately afterward for New York to visit family.

She had bought a new Nikon 8008S that summer and immediately disliked it. She explained why in a 1994 interview with *Western Horseman* magazine.

> I mean, they're fine for certain things. But I don't use the automatic focus because it's just not fast enough. And all that programmed stuff. I can't tell it, "Gee, I'm sorry, but I'm going to have to shoot into the sun." So I still keep my old Nikons, an FA and FM 2. They're totally manual, and I love them.
>
> After having eye surgery sometime back, I thought automatic would be best. But the camera doesn't know if I want to focus on the calf or the calf roper. I want the figures I shoot to be in perfect perspective and exposure. So with the automatic, I end up with everything shutting down much more than I'd shut it down if I were doing it manually.

Louise used Kodak film for her color shots and stuck with Tri-X 400 film for black-and-white prints because she liked its speed.

The new 1,000-speed is too grainy. And I even dilute my developer so that I can minimize the grain on Tri-X.

I want to keep my variables to a minimum and know my equipment inside-out. I just need an extension of my arm and eye. The thing about shooting action, especially in the rodeo ring, is that you never know when and where something is going to happen. You might see it out of the side of your eye, and quickly, you just turn around and take it. Your shot could be into the sun, where a lens hood helps, or it could be in deep shade. It doesn't make any difference. You've got to be ready. If you use the same equipment, if you know it instinctively, then you know what you're doing right or wrong, and can circumvent it in the darkroom. I like to overexpose and under-develop, which is kind of a strange way to go, but it gives me better grade tone.

According to the *Western Horseman* article, Louise was considered one of the best PRCA photographers in the history of the organization.

She was now approaching her sixty-eighth birthday, and again the question of retiring came up, particularly after she heard one young cowboy remark as she climbed into the arena, "What the hell is that old lady doing in the ring?" Still, there were others who preferred to call her "Mom" and looked for her presence at the beginning of each event.

Louise was adamant. "I'm never going to retire. I will retire from the rodeo ring mainly because I cannot move as fast as I used to and that's dangerous to them [the cowboys]. I've got to be able to get out if the way. I've got to be in the right spot at the right time or I have no business being in there. I think thirty years is enough of that. I could not go to a rodeo and not have something to do with it. Either shoot from the sides, something behind the scenes. I'll always do Tucson."

Drawing at least fifty thousand fans during its five-day run, the Tucson Rodeo is "the best outdoor rodeo still going," Louise argued in the *Houston Post* article. "I don't think people realize how lucky they are to have a rodeo of that caliber in Tucson. The people who run it are unbelievable."

The same could be said of Louise, according to rodeo manager Gary Williams, who credits her with making everyone feel as if she had always known them. She also had a good "BS" detector, he says, and although always polite, she would immediately distance herself from people who tried to deceive or cheat her and not allow them into her life.

Gary and Louise spent many an afternoon or evening together "just sitting there and talking about anything and everything under the sun. She has done more to promote this [Tucson] rodeo in particular and rodeo in general than anyone I know.

"She really felt that this was her home and we were all her family. We had such a good time together—we laughed. No matter how serious a conversation we were in, somehow we would always end up in stitches."

Of course they were usually sipping some of Louise's favorite tequila while discussing current or rodeo events. She had an extensive collection of the tasty liquor, derived from the blue agave plant, as people constantly presented her with an eclectic or very expensive bottle, but she seldom drank anything but her favorite Jose Cuervo.

"Every Christmas," according to Gary, "she would fix a rack of lamb and would invite the most interesting group of people. It was everybody from cowboys to architects and artists. She moved so easily from one world to the next—did it seamlessly."

Another venture was about to begin for Louise, an endeavor that would propel her back over the last thirty years to collect and sort through her vast collection of rodeo photographs, culminating in a lifetime assemblage of her work.

Chapter 21

I sold the book out every town I went to.

Aperture Foundation, Inc., has been around since 1952, publishing innovative and inspiring books on photography created by some of the best photojournalists of the day. On July 20, 1993, Louise signed a contract with Aperture to produce a book of her rodeo photographs, aptly titled *Rodeo*.

She worked with editor Melissa Harris to select the photographs for the book. Melissa found Louise stunning, interesting, self-confident, and self-assured; she had "a great sense of humor and she wasn't arrogant or cocky at all, but she really believed in her photographs.

"I remember spending hours and hours and hours talking to her and learning more about rodeo than I ever did in my entire life."

Because Louise still had family in New York, she usually met with her editor there, although Melissa did make at least one trip west to discuss in detail the text of the book. She stayed with Louise at her ranch in Vail. Good thing she did, because, according to Melissa, Louise "made me the strongest margarita I have ever had in my life."

The cover photograph of *Rodeo* shows teenager Matt Martin with a concerned look on his face but in good form at the 1974 high school rodeo in Douglas, Arizona, riding atop a wild-eyed, rather irritated-looking steer as onlookers in the background carefully scrutinize Matt's expertise. He is in the process of losing his hat. Louise did not want this photograph on the cover, as she felt the first picture should be of a professional rodeo rider, not an amateur. The publishers disagreed, insisting this was one of her more expressive pictures and would catch the reader's eye, although her editor admits someone at Aperture removed what was thought to be a spot on the photograph. Turned out to be part of the picture—spit from the cow.

Louise relented to the wishes of her publishers. It was not the last time she came away from a discussion with Aperture disillusioned with the publishing process.

The selection of photos for the book started with some of Louise's first images from 1963. She snapped *Skeeter in the Dust* in 1964 followed by *Cotton Eye*, which she captured in 1989. A picture of cowboy Clay West she titled *Miscalculation* illustrates what can happen when a rider fails to correctly grab a steer's horns during a steer-wrestling contest, while the picture of Kim Roberts working his steer at the Tucson Rodeo in 1985 depicts the accurate form for grabbing onto the animal while sliding sideways off a horse, digging in one's heels, and twisting the steer over the horn.

She shot a dramatic photograph of bronc rider Gerald Farr struggling on his horse, Widow Maker, as it tried to climb the chute at the 1963 Ajo rodeo; it vividly portrays the dangers cowboys face every time they enter the arena, as does a picture of David Thompson attempting to stay on board his horse at the Tucson Rodeo in 1973. In the latter the faces of concerned onlookers peer down as horse and rider both struggle to gain dominance even before they make it into the arena.

The Butt of Lewis Feild was a picture she took behind the chutes at the 1984 ProRodeo Cowboys Association competition

Gerald Farr on Widow Maker, 1963, Arizona Rodeo Association,
Ajo, Arizona

in Yuma. *Hindsight* shows a row of cowboy posteriors watching the action at the 1986 Tucson Rodeo. She took some flak for this picture when it appeared in a February 19, 2005, *Tucson Citizen* article. One reader proffered that Louise "was enamored with the rear view of each cowboy and took the picture to exhibit several male 'hind-quarters.'" The male critic went on to argue that if a man had taken a shot of female cheerleaders' rear ends, the photographer would have been reprimanded because so-called "'equal' standards still put the male gender at a further disadvantage."

Enraged over the criticism of her mother's picture, daughter Mia shot off a scathing letter to the *Citizen* chastising the letter writer and explaining that what he found offensive was, in fact, art. If the reader had "spent any time at a rodeo," she wrote, "he would see that it is common for a group of cowboys to be lined up against a fence watching the competition." Mia argued her mother had spent over forty years perfecting her craft as a rodeo photographer in a male-dominated profession and if the reader really believed men were at a disadvantage when it came to shooting the rear ends of anyone, then he should "Cowboy up!"

As she did with artist Ted DeGrazia back in 1966, Louise captured the weathered hands of bareback rider Chuck Logue as he adjusted his riggings at the 1984 Tucson Rodeo, and the hands of Matthew Terrence tightening the leather string around the wrist of his glove at the Yuma Rodeo that same year. The anguished look on Travis Howe's face as he removed the tape from his gloves after competing in the 1983 Turquoise Circuit Finals in Tucson may indicate a not-so-successful ride.

She always preferred candid shots to posed pictures, and included in *Rodeo* two images of cowboys who seemed oblivious to her presence, one shot in 1993 at the Turquoise Finals when she came upon a group of cowboys limbering up behind the chutes before heading into the arena, and another cowboy cluster waiting their turn to ride at the Calgary, Alberta, Canada rodeo in 1983.

She photographed barrel racer Twila Hamman, horse and rider in great form careening around barrels at the 1968 Arizona Junior Rodeo in Globe, as well as Kay Vamvoras at another Globe rodeo in 1983.

In pictures of rodeo clown Jeff Kobza, Louise detailed the dangers still prevalent after a cowboy had a good ride and left the arena. She caught Jeff just before a bull did at the Yuma Rodeo in 1983, and in 1984 at the Buckeye Rodeo she was right there when a bull tossed Jeff over its shoulder.

Amazing shots of a 1983 chuck wagon race in Calgary and a wild horse race at the Prescott Rodeo in 1984 make it seem as if she was right on the track as the horses pounded around the course.

She captured the features of cowboys deep in concentration, displaying a myriad of emotions—some are angry, while others show determination, frustration, the agony of a bad ride, or the sheer joy of completing a hard-ridden competition.

Her photographs of juvenile rodeo participants bravely hanging on to skittish calves also showcase reactions from fear to utter delight. She caught little Yates Dixon with a determined look, arm high in the air as he rode his first calf at the 1983 Cowpunchers Reunion in Williams, Arizona. Cole Gould's father is shown brushing off his son and checking him for injuries after a bout with a calf at the same rodeo.

Still carrying a torch for the cowboy who got away, Louise dedicated *Rodeo* to Lex Connelly, "who imbued me with his love of rodeo fifty years ago." She also included photographer Bruce Weber in her dedication, saying that his "generosity of spirit and support opened doors to the outside world."

She was not at all pleased with the preface that western author Larry McMurtry was asked to write for the book.

"I don't know why they had McMurtry write anything," she told a reporter for *Southwest Art*. "He hates rodeos. I guess they thought it would sell books."

Melissa and Louise debated the inclusion of McMurtry's words, with the Aperture editor winning the argument. It was not a heated discussion, according to Melissa, but just two people coming from very different perspectives. "Editorially for us," she says, "having this kind of counterpoint, and it's very well written, interesting, and funny . . . it made the book more interesting. But she [Louise] was so romantic about rodeo."

Melissa also reasoned that the book was not being published to promote rodeo but to promote Louise's talents as a photographer, and that McMurtry's dislike of rodeo would add tension to the manuscript.

McMurtry did praise Louise's work in his essay but proclaimed that rodeo was nothing more than "show biz—its relation to ranch work is oblique at best. . . . I don't admire rodeo," he said, "whereas Ms. Serpa loves it." While lauding Louise's photography skills, a 1994 *Houston Post* article claimed McMurtry proffered that "a rodeo cowboy is not a cowboy at all but a showman, that the West of Cowboys and cattle is all but dead."

When she read his remarks, Louise reacted. "I was furious. I love rodeo, and I love these people, and that's a very belittling piece."

In a letter to her editor, she expressed her distaste with McMurtry's words.

"Why Larry is so embittered about the West I don't know and it's his business anyway but I'm sorry he finds it necessary to insult the intelligence of anyone connected with the soil, livestock or rodeo. There is so much that is uplifting, rewarding, difficult at times, yes but steadfast. I wouldn't trade the west for anything or anywhere."

In another letter to her editor, Louise continued her tirade against using McMurtry's words:

> *Larry, as a person, I like from what little I've seen. I would like to see him (without a third person present) alone at leisure and philosophize a bit so I know why he's so bitter & dene-grading [sic] about the west in general and so he can appreci-ate all the positive things the west has supplied me through 42 years of hard work not just in rodeo.*
>
> *If "tension" is what you want, you've got it, from me at least. Nothing anyone can say will make me feel good about this essay or even that it's well written (and I like very much most of what Larry has written before). But you are the pub-lishers—I'll just sink back to what I know best—the photo-graphs.*

She insisted that his comments not be used in the preface or introduction but relegated to the last pages of the book, "with not one recognizable cowboy picture next to it."

McMurtry's words, however, appear just before the last three photographs in the book, which infuriated Louise even more.

"Instead of closing the gap re the completion of the book," she wrote her editor, "I feel it is getting wider and totally out of my control. Somebody misunderstood me about Larry's text. I hate it now as I have always hated it since my first message to you on your answering machine. I let myself be talked into let-ting it be (which I should not have) on the understanding that it be at the end of the book and that to my mind means after all pictures."

After sending off final edits of the manuscript in the spring of 1994, Louise needed to clear her head of the entire project. She set off that summer, alone and unencumbered, on a ten-day driving tour to Bruce Weber's place in Montana. Bruce had advised her not to do the book, but Louise argued she needed to produce this photographic presentation of her work because it revealed who she was; it was part of her history.

She traveled through northern Arizona before stopping in Las Vegas, where she said she caught some type of "tummy bug in the middle of the night." By the time she reached Idaho, her stomach was no better but she determined nothing as minor as a bellyache was going to ruin her solitary road trip.

She stopped at a donkey farm in the Idaho Sawtooth Mountains to take a few photographs and arrived at Bruce's ranch in time to make an appearance at the Danforth Gallery exhibition in Livingston that August.

After celebrating the success of the show with Bruce, she started home, wandering through Montana's Crazy Mountains, which she described as "splendid," before moseying down through Wyoming and into the Colorado town of Hot Sulphur Springs, where Native Americans used to camp and utilize the hot springs for medicinal purposes. She wandered through New Mexico's Gila Wilderness just north of Silver City, where she encountered some deadly-looking storms that held little rain, before heading west into Arizona.

When she arrived home the finished book was waiting for her, and she pronounced the final product "not too bad."

Although Aperture rarely scheduled book tours, the publicity team felt Louise's dynamic personality would certainly garner attention on the road. They arranged a promotional circuit even though the publisher of Aperture, Roger Strauss III, expressed doubts that a rodeo book would sell well. "I sincerely think he's wrong," Louise wrote to her editor. "The response I've had from Europe—Germany in particular is so strong! The Germans, French & Japanese are enormous rodeo fans—it's almost an addiction and to my knowledge there is no other good rodeo action book out."

Tightly clutching the new book under her arm, Louise could not have asked for more appreciative audiences wherever she went. "They put me on the road with the book and it was great," she told reporter Betty Barr. "I'd never done it before and I sold the book out every town I went to."

In April 1995 *Rodeo* was selected as one of fifty books to win the prestigious American Institute of Graphic Arts Design of the Year award.

Roger Strauss resigned as publisher of Aperture in July 1994 after only eight months on the job.

Chapter 22

There is always something somewhere happening in the arena.

Just before setting out on her book tour, Louise was asked to put together a display of her work from the beginning of her career to the present to be shown at the Tucson Museum of Art. In December 1994 the retrospective *30 Years in the Arena* opened, with Louise reigning as the "grande dame" of rodeo photography, even though she continuously insisted, "I just shoot what I like. If someone else likes it, more the better."

News shows began calling, wanting to interview the popular rodeo photographer. Her calendar indicated she was interviewed by television journalist Charles Kuralt, probably for one of his famous *On the Road* segments that aired on the CBS Evening News for over twenty years. She also noted she did a taping for the NPR radio show *All Things Considered* that aired in November 1994.

Television newscaster Tom Brokaw asked her to photograph his West Boulder Ranch in Montana. She had met Brokaw on one of her visits to Bruce Weber's ranch, as Brokaw's ranch was nearby. A note Brokaw wrote October 12, 1994, shows his appreciation of her work. "Thank you for your wonderful reminder

Louise at the Tucson Rodeo in 1995
COURTESY OF HUBERT PEFFER

of a glorious summer. Memories of the real Boulder will get us through NY winters!"

She flew to New York to be interviewed on WNYC-TV and to attend the opening of one of Bruce's shows, then back to Las Vegas to appear on the *Good Morning Las Vegas* TV show before dashing over to Neiman Marcus for a book signing.

Television and radio requests poured in. She appeared on Tucson's local PBS TV news show *Arizona Illustrated* in January 1995 to discuss her exhibit at the Tucson Museum of Art. That same month, the city of Tucson TV station interviewed her on its *Voices of Tucson* show, where she boasted she had a complete file on everything she had ever shot. She claimed she had taken over seventy-eight hundred rolls of film, each with thirty-six exposures, and that she had saved every image she had photographed on a proof sheet with information about the rodeo at which the picture was shot, the names of the horse and rider in the picture, and what the cowboy scored on the ride.

As she proffered in her book *Rodeo*, "After thirty-five years being a part of it [the rodeo], I still get the adrenaline surge, feel the excitement, the warmth of old friendship; I still anticipate the action, and wonder if I can be in the right place at the right time with the camera focused. From the photographer's point of view, rodeo is never static: no two rides are ever the same, and there is no time for a lag in concentration. It gives me a real charge. There is always something somewhere happening in the arena."

She was in the wrong place at the wrong time that January, however, when she wrecked her car and ended up in bed from severe shock. And she learned the hard way that she was not immune from scorpion bites when she discovered that fall she had sustained what she called a "double bite" from one of these varmints. But none of these incidents kept her down for long. As with most of the injuries she sustained throughout her career, these were minor disturbances that faded in time for her to be on the road to the next rodeo.

In the spring of 1995 *Vassar Quarterly*, the alumnae/i magazine of Vassar College, published an article about its famous alumna, describing Louise as a rebel and praising her success in the rodeo arena since her graduation. "Wearing a broad-brimmed cowboy hat and shiny boots," the article started out, "her skin tawny and creased from years spent outdoors, Louise Larocque Serpa '46 was easy to spot in midtown Manhattan. The woman who for thirty-five years has made a living photographing rodeos looks like a portrait of the American West."

"While dodging bulls and bucking broncs," the article continued, "Serpa stops the action in midair with her camera, shooting photos that jump off the page. The action is so close you can practically hear the grunts of bulls and cowboys and feel the dust choking your lungs."

The author quoted Louise as saying she had no intention of retiring. "She still feels the jolt of adrenaline when she steps into

Louise at the Tucson Rodeo, circa 1995

the arena, a surge that makes her feel young. She feels a great sense of accomplishment from capturing three generations of cowboys on film."

The reaction to the article was anything but complimentary. Several letters to the editor commented on the cruelty of the sport, how animals were abused for the pleasure of stoking a few male egos.

"Far from being an American—or western—tradition, modern rodeos exhibit skills almost totally irrelevant to cowboy activities past or present," wrote one critic. "We have seen the calf slammed against the steel fence, breaking his nose, bleeding, falling down, yet lassoed all the same, then left in the sun for six hours before being hauled off to the slaughterhouse.

"My concern and disgust has to do primarily with the abuse of animals, but it is highly ironic that Vassar, that bastion of women's independence and welfare, should associate itself in any way with this sexist, macho 'sport.'" The writer went on to quote from Elizabeth Atwood Lawrence's book *Rodeo: An Anthropologist Looks at the Wild and the Tame*, in which Lawrence recorded a champion steer wrestler saying, "Women should not rodeo any more than men can have babies. Women were put on earth to reproduce, and are close to animals. Women's liberation is on an equal to gay liberation—they both are ridiculous."

"If Mrs. Serpa were really a rebel," wrote another alumnus, "she would recognize that rodeo is nothing but a barbaric ritual of domination designed to feed the egos and wallets of humans. . . . In short, she would find a career that doesn't depend upon the brutalization of her fellow creatures."

One of the first to respond to these hostile remarks about Louise and rodeo was Terri Greer, animal welfare director of the Professional Rodeo Cowboys Association. Ms. Greer wrote to the editor of the *Vassar Quarterly*:

Of all the people qualified to judge if any abuse to animals exists in professional rodeos, Louise would certainly be far more reliable . . . Louise has been there, literally thousands of times. These ladies have not.

The sport of professional rodeo simply will not tolerate inhumane treatment of its animal athletes. Sixty rules govern their protection.

To Louise, we say, although someone has taken the opportunity to hurt you by thoughtless deeds on the heels of such a well written article, we want you to know you have our thoughts, our well wishes, and most importantly, our hope that you realize individuals such as these, thankfully, do not represent the majority of Americans or the majority of women for that matter.

Louise had always maintained that because rodeo animals were the lifeblood of those who owned them, they were "the most pampered, well-cared-for bulls and horses you ever saw in your life," as she told a reporter for *Southwest Art*, "well-bedded and well-vetted."

In her 1995 television interview she remained adamant that rodeo continued to be "the most wonderful occupation, profession, whatever you want to call it, that anybody could get into."

Following the tumult the Vassar article provoked, Louise headed back to Montana that summer for another show with Bruce Weber at the Danforth Gallery. This time she traveled by way of Santa Fe, Denver, and Yellowstone before arriving in Livingston, Montana.

The exhibit that year was promoted as pictures taken by the "Montana Photo Gang," consisting of Louise's photographs as well as those of Bruce Weber, self-taught Montana photographer Kurt Markus, and another native Montanan, fashion and art photographer Paul Jasmin. An unsigned letter from the gallery to Louise explained that the Park County Friends of the Arts, sponsor of the exhibit, was a nonprofit community art center, and that artists were not selected on the salability of their art but for the quality of their work.

The letter went on to state that the gallery was "absolutely ecstatic about the success" of the show. "The opening reception was packed to maximum capacity! . . . everyone enjoyed themselves, the artwork, and the company. Throughout the show, we had visitors from across the state who had driven long hours for the purpose of seeing the exhibition." Louise sold at least seven of her pictures, with a percentage of each sale going to the Park County Friends of the Arts.

Leaving Livingston, she stopped at a rodeo in Choteau, Montana, before driving home via the coastline, visiting her old homestead in Ashland, Oregon.

That November she gave a lecture at Southern Utah University (SUU). "Thirty Years in the Arena" offered tips to aspiring photojournalists about the craft of photography. In introducing Louise, Lana Johnson, SUU's director of lectures and special projects, quoted a writer who had recently published an article about Louise, affirming that her forthright personality was "not surprising, since the better part of her 70 years has been spent in the dusty arena, where pretense is regarded as so much cow dung." Louise's talk was a huge success.

The day after her speech, she opened an exhibit of her work at the Braithwaite Fine Arts Gallery on the university campus, featuring her black-and-white rodeo pictures as well as some of her scenic images of Montana.

Chapter 23

It's time to go back to civilization.

O nce her book *Rodeo* was launched and selling well, Louise
settled back into the routine of traipsing from one rodeo to
another. She detoured in early 1996 to drive through the pictur-
esque Muleshoe Ranch Cooperative Management Area located
in southeastern Arizona's Galiuro Mountains. More than forty-
nine thousand acres sit between the Sonoran and Chihuahuan
Deserts and consist of semidesert grasslands undisturbed by
modern-day hubbub, serving as a preservation area for the sur-
rounding ecosystems as well as desert wildlife.

From Muleshoe she drove the circuitous route through
Elfrida and Portal before crossing into New Mexico to visit
the town of Rodeo, and headed home by way of Willcox, Arizona.

Louise did not detail what this jaunt encompassed, but
she might have been trying to clear her head for an upcoming
national interview on PBS, the Public Broadcasting System.

The documentary *When the Dust Settles* first aired in May
1996 and continues to be shown today. It is a comprehensive
view of Louise's life and profession, her love of rodeos and the
cowboys who adopted her into their lifestyle, and her lifelong
love affair with the camera.

She appears nervous at the beginning of the interview, which was shot at her X9 Ranch. Her short, salt-and-pepper hair bounces about her tanned, weathered face while her hazel brown eyes dart uneasily as she tries to focus on the camera and the interviewer at the same time. Within minutes however, after her clothes dryer buzzer goes off unexpectedly during the filming, those deep laugh lines appear around her mouth and eyes, so prevalent in photographs of her, and she settles into a comfortable camaraderie with the film crew, discussing rodeos, cowboys, and cameras, topics she could expound on for hours.

"Rodeo is a fraternity," she said in the documentary. "Each person who rides will share the knowledge he has had with a particular horse with the next person who draws it, and that's an unusual thing in itself."

"There's a camaraderie, there's an acceptance, there's a lack of being able to take yourself seriously—they [the cowboys] won't let you."

She spoke of her ongoing affection for the camera. "The one thing I have been left with besides the love of rodeo and everybody connected with it, and we'll always have that, is the love of the camera and love of being able to look at lightness and darkness and trying to figure out how you can get the optimum out of whatever you're given."

An article that appeared in the *Arizona Daily Star* just before the debut of the documentary described Louise as a woman who "had to get close, draw fast and shoot straight."

"And in the arena," Louise said, "you never know where the action is going to be, so the ability to shoot from the hip and shoot fast comes in handy."

Shortly after completing the filming of *When the Dust Settles*, she went to New York to attend her fiftieth reunion at Vassar. She held no grudge against the critics who had censured her profession the year before in the school's magazine.

That fall she took her usual excursion to Montana, where she noted on her calendar that she "popped a hamstring" while waterskiing. She was now seventy years old, yet still frolicked with the rest of the adolescents.

From Montana she made her way to Pendleton, Oregon, to photograph the Pendleton Roundup, but was back in Arizona to shoot the Willcox rodeo in October and the Turquoise Finals in Bullhead City that November.

Yet something else was occupying Louise's thoughts throughout her travels, disturbing her peace of mind—the time had come to leave her beloved X9 Ranch. She was concerned that if she fell or something just as dire happened to her on the ranch, it might be days before anyone found her. She knew she had to move closer to town. Since 1972 she had enjoyed the wildness and isolation of her Rincon Mountains home, but now it presented a danger to her well-being.

"It's just killing me to move into town," she told a *Tucson Citizen* reporter in 1997. "But I can't hike the way I used to. If I fall down, I'm in trouble. It's time to go back to civilization."

According to Gary Williams, it was at one of the Tucson Rodeos in the late 1990s that Louise happened to pass by Pat Manley, owner of the Johnson Manley Lumber Company in Tucson. They were both circling the arena on horseback during the grand entry of contestants. For years Pat had owned land in the old Fort Lowell area on the eastern end of town. Originally this expanse of land was known as the Douglas Farm, owned by Lewis Williams Douglas (1894–1974), who had been a politician on the local and national level (1922–33), ambassador to Great Britain (1947–50), and a noted Arizona banker.

But long before Douglas discovered this prime piece of real estate, the ancient Hohokam people knew the area contained an abundance of ground water that would sustain their crops in even the driest years. Hohokam pottery shards can still be found sparsely scattered across these lands.

The Fort Lowell military post was established on this acreage from 1873 to 1891 to protect settlers from raiding Apaches who had used the waterways unencumbered until the onset of settlers forced them off the land. Mexican farmers and ranchers moved into the area after the military abandoned Fort Lowell, once again taking advantage of the Rillito River waters and the confluence of Tanque Verde and Pantano Creeks to quench the thirst of their livestock, their crops, and their families.

Because of the eclectic mix of cultural and racial families who had lived on this extensive stretch of land for centuries, the area was placed on the National Register of Historic Places in 1978, and the city of Tucson titled portions of the region the Fort Lowell Historic Area in 1981.

With an abundance of vegetation, woodland, and wildlife within arm's reach of the amenities Louise was seeking, the Fort Lowell district was the perfect spot for an aging cowgirl who was having trouble letting go of her independence.

As Gary recalls, she continued to circle the arena that February day, waving to the crowd. Passing by Pat Manley, she leaned over her horse and asked him if he knew of any good land for sale. The two again trotted around the ring in opposite directions. Meeting up again, Pat mentioned he had some acreage next to his property in the Fort Lowell district that he would be happy to sell her. It might have taken a few more rounds of the arena grounds, but the two struck a deal that day that Louise would buy some of Pat's property. How appropriate she found her next home while circling the rodeo arena.

In late 1996 Louise put her X9 property on the market. Advertised as horse property in a prestigious gated community, surrounded on three sides by Saguaro National Park's Rincon Mountain ranges, the thirty-nine-hundred-square-foot house was touted as a secluded paradise just twenty-five miles from Tucson. By the end of the year, she had a buyer.

"When I sold my last place [the X9 Ranch house]," she said in an interview with *Tucson Lifestyle* in 2005, "which had 40 acres of land up against the wilderness, I cried every day for about a year." She would sorely miss the seclusion and grandeur of this magnificent house, but she was already hard at work designing her new home.

"I need a house that I can live in every part of," she said, "where there is no waste. And one thing I did not want was a house where you had to plump pillows after you get up. I want to put my feet up on anything and not worry about it."

The Fort Lowell house was designed by architect Bob Taylor, with Louise serving as interior designer and landscaper, something she may have learned at the knees of her interior designer mother.

She and Bob positioned the house to achieve the best possible views of the Santa Catalina and Rincon Mountains. The sometimes babbling Rillito River flowed nearby.

She painted the massive great room with what one reporter described as the color of aged saddle leather. The high tongue-in-grove ceiling trusses were constructed of pickled pine to complement furniture she had purchased over the years, such as an antique English corner library chair and a coffee table designed from the hatch cover of a whaling ship. In her simplistic style she refused to use bedspreads because, she said, "you just have to undo them."

Her rodeo photographs dominated a long, wide hallway leading to her darkroom. Stunning pictures she had taken of African antelopes and the Australian countryside dotted the rest of the house.

"It is amazing what you can do if you put your money into a house and don't spend it on frivolous things," she said, but she was not frugal when it came to purchasing what she wanted, such as the baby grand piano she bought so she could sing whenever she wished. And just outside the front door, she built a fountain that her future grandson Taylor would use for his goldfish when they outgrew their tank. "We put in green things," Louise said, "to make it ecologically sound, and tested it first with mosquito fish. Finally we added the goldfish with great ceremony, and two days later there were only two of them. Three days later, there were none, but there were raccoons walking around my property who were very happy and well-fed."

She moved into her new abode in September 1997, but the months prior to her move were anything but idle.

She shot the Scottsdale and Yuma rodeos before the annual February roundup in Tucson. During that competition she was interviewed by NBC for an appearance on the early-morning show *Today*. For two days television crews followed her every move around the arena grounds. "They came back for one more day," she said in a *Houston Post* interview, "because they didn't get the picture they wanted, which was basically me being challenged by a bull. And they sure got it the last day."

Even Bruce Weber was interviewed about his friendship and business relationship with Louise for the program.

Before the show aired she once again took off on a trek around the globe to shoot the Royal Easter Show in Sydney, Australia, the last time she would see the wonders of a land she had grown to love.

The NBC crew returned in April for additional material, and in June the *Today* interview aired.

Louise had been in New York just prior to her *Today* appearance and had the unfortunate experience of having her Nikon FM 2 camera stolen, a disaster for any photographer. It was never found.

Chapter 24

I don't go anywhere without a camera.

Comfortably settled in her new Fort Lowell home, Louise shot the Turquoise Circuit in Prescott in January 1998, just prior to the Tucson Rodeo. With her photographs now selling for as much as $2,000, she had cameras stashed around her home, in her car, and always somewhere on her body.

"I don't go anywhere without a camera," she told a reporter for *Taylor Talk* in 1998. "Most of the time, I have a camera loaded with black-and-white in my car. I always keep one in my purse, too. That way, if a snake does something extraordinary, I can shoot it." The day a couple of rattlesnakes decided to mate outside her window at the X9 Ranch house, she was a brazen observer of the ritual, shooting the rare sight with one of her nearby, ever-ready cameras.

That summer she made one of her solo treks through Sedona, Santa Fe, and Colorado Springs, on her way to a one-man show of her work at the Holter Museum of Art in Helena, Montana, which also featured her book *Rodeo*. Returning through Pine Bluffs, Wyoming, and still energetic as ever, she had the opportunity to herd cattle with an old friend before heading home.

Since 1992 Louise had delighted in the antics of a female Timneh African grey parrot that originally had belonged to her daughter Mia. Hatari became a constant companion for Louise—they sang together, particularly opera, and even showered together. Birds of that species do not like to be confined in cages, and Hatari was no exception. Louise refused to clip the parrot's wings, giving it free range of the entire house.

Considered one of the most intelligent birds, the Timneh African grey parrot is smaller than its neighboring relative the Congo grey parrot, growing only about ten inches and weighing under a pound. Some have lived as long as fifty years. The species is usually charcoal-grey with a deep pink or coral beak and sports a dark-burgundy-colored tail. It thrives in western regions of Africa and is a popular pet because of its intelligence and ability to imitate human speech as well as other sounds, such as whistles, alarms, even video game noises. Some estimate the parrot's intelligence to be similar to a five-year-old child, while its temperament is more like that of a two-year-old.

Hatari would seek out Louise, walk or fly up to her while she was busily proofing or developing pictures, and inquisitively ask, "Whatcha doing?"

Like its owner, the parrot favored tequila as its drink of choice, especially tequila sunrises made with orange juice and grenadine.

One day Louise strolled down the lane of her house to fetch the mail, a rather long walk. As she sauntered along she looked down to see a $20 bill at her feet. She walked a little farther and found another $20 bill. By the time she reached her mailbox, she had a whole fistful of cash. Her first thought was that it was drug money. Louise called Mia and asked what she should do with these ill-gotten funds. Mia laughingly told her mother she should go out walking again tomorrow—who knows what she might find!

Instead the two decided to go to Mexico and spend it on a good meal. Afterward they wandered the streets of Nogales, admiring the wares for sale, and came upon a beautiful cage they thought perfect for Hatari. Although grey parrots dislike the confinement of a cage, they do prefer a home base in which to eat, play with their toys, and generally feel safe. Hence the money Louise found on her property was used to bring a little peace and quiet to the Serpa household, particularly since, along with ten-year-old Hatari, Louise had two springer spaniel dogs, Angus and Meggie, running around the house. She found dogs great companions and thought the world of all the dogs she owned through the years. They were her closest companions no matter what, or who, might discombobulate her life.

Meggie was about six months old and still full of puppy playfulness. Every morning at four o'clock, the excited pooch nudged Louise awake, eager for their walk along the trail that rambled beside the Rillito River.

One particular October day Louise took advantage of an exceptionally balmy weather forecast to work outside. With her dogs safely ensconced inside the house, she was free to roam without worrying where the two curious canines might run off to or what they unexpectedly might find in the desert wash. She heard Hatari squawking inside, which the bird did occasionally, and thought nothing of it. *He probably needs some attention*, Louise might have thought. Not until she went inside and saw feathers strewn down the hallway did she get a sick feeling something was wrong. She found Hatari dead on the floor. Meggie had not killed the parrot, but Louise thought the young, excitable dog had probably scared Hatari to death.

Devastated, Louise knew Meggie had not purposely harmed Hatari. She saw no reason to ban the woeful puppy because of its youthful yet disastrous indiscretion. So she forgave the forlorn pooch and the two contentedly lived the remainder of their days together.

Taylor Grammar as mutton buster, age five

Louise's life was abruptly and delightfully enriched on February 3, 1998, when Taylor Joseph Grammar was born to her daughter Lauren. Louise doted on young Taylor, even noting on her calendar the date she first babysat him.

"Gran," as Taylor called his grandmother, soon had her young grandson totally immersed in the Tucson Rodeo. He took to clowning and mutton bustin' at the age of three, and for the next five years he helped small fry climb onto sheep or calves and gently picked them up and dusted them off after a bumpy ride.

When he was not performing he hung out with his grandmother, if she was not busy in the arena. She made sure he knew how to ride at an early age, and he spent as much time as possible with her both at the rodeo and in her home. When his sixth-grade class planned a trip to Spain, Portugal, and Morocco, she paid his way, hoping the sights and the experiences he would encounter might stay with him and maybe endow him with the wanderlust his grandmother so enjoyed.

Taylor is now a handsome, strapping teenager who prefers football gear to clown costumes. He greatly misses his grandmother but still likes to go to the rodeo, admitting it is not as much fun as when Gran was there taking pictures of the action and, of course, of him.

Lauren and Taylor's father, John Grammar, had married in March 1998, but the couple divorced about a year later.

When Tucson's local television channel KOLD came out to her house for an interview in early 1999 in preparation for the opening of the Tucson Rodeo, Louise was just returning from the Turquoise Circuit Finals and in the process of putting together a show for the Mountain Oyster Club, scheduled to debut February 19, just days before the rodeo parade.

The Mountain Oyster Club had moved since its inception in 1948 at Tucson's Santa Rita Hotel, now holding its meetings, dinners, and art shows in an old adobe building on the corner of Stone and Franklin Streets in the historic district of downtown Tucson. The club, whose motto has always been *Cerveza y huevos para todos* (beer and eggs for all), remained in these digs from 1975 until it moved again in 2004. Louise was a member for at least twenty years.

Each fall the club sponsors the Annual Southwestern Art Show and Sale, considered one of the best showcases for western art. Louise's February show was a one-artist exhibition of her rodeo photographs.

Once she had the display up and running, it was time to hike up her jeans, strap on her cameras, and head for the rodeo grounds. Having celebrated her seventy-third birthday the previous December, she still refused to consider retiring, "as long as I don't get in the way," she told a reporter for the *Mercedes Momentum* in 1998, "and as long as I can get the job done. I tried to quit for about six months, but I just flat-out missed it."

"I will do Tucson until I drop," she insisted.

Chapter 25

You stagger me.

In April 1999 Louise underwent additional surgery on her hand for the incident involving the bull she had tried to run over on her way home to Vail years earlier. In June she came down with the flu, which left her flat on her back for a few days, and in July her old dog Angus was bitten by a snake.

By August she and Angus were both back on their feet in time for Louise to be interviewed by *ProRodeo Sports News*. The National Cowgirl Hall of Fame in Fort Worth, Texas, had just announced its inductees for 1999, and Louise was stunned she was one of them. Newspapers, magazines, and talk shows clamored for interviews.

"It was a total surprise," she said in an October *ProRodeo Sports News* article. "It's an enormous tribute, and it just came out of left field."

The article also mentioned that she considered her one obligation was to shoot the annual Tucson Rodeo, although she had admitted just a few months earlier that she still photographed "cowpuncher rodeos, work[ed] the Williams rodeo in the summer and [did] a lot of ranch work."

"This [the upcoming 2000 Tucson Rodeo] will be my last one," she said. "It's Tucson's 75th anniversary and I'll turn 75 later in the year, and it just seems like a good time to quit."

Having never photographed or even attended a women's rodeo, Louise was not familiar with the National Cowgirl Hall of Fame—not "until I got down there and really saw the caliber of women I was going in with or would be associated with," she remembered during her 2004 interview with the Rodeo Historical Society. "That was fabulous."

She felt humbled to be included with that year's other inductees—bronc rider Bertha Blancett; trainer, judge, and top quarter horse breeder Suzanne Norton Jones; and horse racing's top female jockey, Julie Krone.

On October 28 at Fort Worth's Worthington Hotel, Louise, wearing the western hat she had acquired for the launch of her book *Rodeo* a few years prior, made her way onstage. She spoke before a crowd of over seven hundred western aficionados, obviously astonished and thrilled to be there.

> *I'm staggered. I have faced lots of bulls and horses and things in the arena that have happened that I wasn't expecting to face, and coped with it, but you stagger me.*
>
> *Being inducted into this extraordinary place has got to be the pinnacle for me . . . Every time I could do anything that related to rodeo—with a camera because that was the only thing I knew how to do—I got closer to the people involved. If I could take a picture of hands or horses or anything that was the backbone of what we still think of as the West, that's where my heart was . . .*
>
> *All the families that were involved in rodeo or horse shows or cutting . . . they accepted me, which was the greatest gift until today that I could have. I was accepted for what I could do and as a person, and it was just wonderful.*
>
> *It has been the most wonderful forty years.*

M. Scott Skinner of the *Arizona Daily Star* caught up with Louise shortly after her return from Fort Worth. With a laugh that is captured in the photograph accompanying the article, she told the reporter who asked about her lengthy, successful career, "I wasn't trying to be the first woman anything. It just happened."

She described the induction ceremony as "mind-boggling. I had no idea how big a deal it was, and the caliber of people I was inducted with . . . what a tough bunch of wonderful dames."

Tucson's Northern Trust Bank of Arizona and the Tubac Art Museum both held showings of Louise's work during this busy time. She also reconnected with one-time rodeo queen Charlotte (Quihuis) Bell.

As a student at the University of Arizona during the early 1960s, Charlotte entered the rodeo arena competing in calf roping and barrel racing, with Louise taking pictures of her on several occasions. In 1963 she garnered the title Miss Rodeo Arizona, and the following year she donned the Tucson Rodeo Queen sash.

Charlotte left Arizona for several years but returned to open the Graham Bell Gallery in Tubac's flourishing art community. In 1999 she asked Louise if she could sell her pictures at the gallery. At her openings Charlotte usually featured country and western singers and copious amounts of food, wine, and soft drinks. Louise, who usually came with her own bottle of tequila, was often found out in the alley, chatting with the cowboys.

Charlotte had almost annual showings of Louise's pictures for the next six or seven years. One year Gary Williams came with Louise to the opening only to find that wine was the only libation on the premises. Knowing Louise's penchant for tequila, Gary walked down to the local cantina and brought back a couple of shots, keeping Louise content for the evening.

"She was a lady," Charlotte says. She never flirted with the cowboys and did not pretend to be anything she wasn't. "If she didn't like you, she would tell you." Charlotte called her a female John Wayne because even though she dressed as a cow-girl, there was a certain look about her that made a person stand back and admire her poise and demeanor.

Gary once said of Louise, "In a dirty pair of jeans, she'd still be the classiest person you'd ever run into."

Chapter 26

I can't imagine not having a camera
with me all the time.

In the spring of 2000, journalist and author Betty Barr, who
was working with the Sonoita (Arizona) Quarter Horse Show
Committee, invited Louise to be part of the program because
of her involvement in photographing performances for many
years. That year the event was to receive historic recognition
from the American Quarter Horse Association. From that first
meeting, Louise and Betty became friends and working part-
ners, roaming across southern Arizona photographing and
writing about historic ranches and the people who were trying desperately to preserve a vanishing lifestyle. "There is no
money to be made in cattle anymore," Louise said, "unless you
have backing from somewhere else."

Louise had loved ranching since she lived in Oregon in the
1950s. "If I had not gotten divorced when I got divorced, and
had two babies," she said in her 1995 television interview, "I
would still be ranching in Oregon. I'd rather do that than anything."

For some time she had been contemplating publishing
a book about ranches and ranching. She had an idea to shoot

"fourth-, fifth-, sixth-, seventh-generation ranches that are still in the same hands. And it's getting harder and harder to do" she said in the 1994 *Houston Post* article. She reiterated her concerns in the 2004 *Southwest Art* story. "The West is phasing out of the ranching business. There is so much history behind so many of these people." With her photographer's eye she recognized that "the whole story is in their faces."

Louise and Betty teamed up to write and photograph historic Empire Ranch, situated about fifty miles south of Tucson in the Las Cienegas National Conservation Area and listed on the National Register of Historic Places. Louise had been the honored guest at the ranch's 2002 annual Roundup. While Betty interviewed John Donaldson and his son Mac, who ran the ranch, Louise photographed the men and the property for an article that appeared in *Range* magazine in the summer of 2004.

That fall they worked together on a story about the Bell family, who owned Bear Valley Ranch in Nogales, Arizona, near Pena Blanca Lake in the foothills of the Pajarito Mountains. "Ranching on the Borderlands" also appeared in *Range*. Graham Bell Gallery owners Tom and Charlotte Bell, who have been promoting Louise's photographs for many years in their Tubac gallery, are part of this Bell clan.

About a year into their friendship, Betty wrote a piece about Louise that appeared in the *Sonoita Weekly Bulletin*, detailing her societal background and her love of rodeo and photography.

"She followed the quarter horse show circuit for a long time, starting out in Sonoita," Betty wrote. "By then her prices had risen to $7 [per picture] and she would park her station wagon and tape the proof sheets up in the windows. . . . [I]t was like a marquee!"

The twosome returned to Nogales in October 2004 to write and photograph the Guevavi Ranch, which has been turned into a bed-and-breakfast retreat, Hacienda Corona de Guevavi.

Established in 1691 by Jesuit priest Father Eusebio Francisco Kino as his first mission in the continental United States, the property became the oldest cattle ranch in Arizona when Spanish explorer Juan Bautista de Anza introduced livestock onto this land in the early 1700s.

Owners Phil and Wendy Stover invited Louise and Betty to spend the night at the historic B&B, but Louise had scheduled an early appointment the next day in Tucson and said she had to head home. After spending a delightful cocktail hour with her hosts, she downed her usual shot of tequila and headed out, none the worse for indulging in her favorite beverage.

In May 2005 Louise and Betty interviewed the Wilson family at Falcon Valley Cattle Ranch, about thirty miles north of Tucson in Oracle, Arizona. "The group [of cowboys] worked really well together," Betty remembers, "and [we] had lots of fun doing it. They gave Louise a very large mountain oyster [bull testicle] with fur intact so she could make a purse!" One of the cowboys suggested she dry it and hang it on a doorknob, while the patriarch of the family, Ralph Wilson, brazenly dangled one of the tantalizing sacs from his mouth, bemoaning the fact that his wife Jan refused to kiss him anymore.

According to Betty, "In typical cowboy fashion, the MOs [mountain oysters] were roasted on the branding stove and we all ate them."

This article had been contracted to appear in the 2005 issue of *Western Horseman* magazine. Over a year later, however, the article had not yet been published. Deciding not to run the piece, the magazine paid the two women for their work, and Betty was able to rewrite the article and use Louise's photographs to sell the story to *Range* for its winter 2008 issue. Receiving payment from both publications certainly made this venture a lucrative undertaking for both writer and photographer, and those mountain oysters tasted even sweeter.

Louise was still shooting several rodeos along with the annual Tucson competition. She was in Colorado Springs, Colorado, in August 2000 and made it back in time for the Sonoita rodeo that September. She photographed the National Finals Rodeo in Las Vegas, Nevada, the following year.

"Always something to do with a camera," she fondly recalled during her interview with the Rodeo Historical Society, "and I can't imagine not having a camera with me all the time."

She was also busy with exhibits of her work, more so since her book *Rodeo* had come out. She followed a summer 2000 exhibition in Sedona with the opening of a show at Tubac's Graham Bell Gallery the following year. She appeared in Wickenburg at the Desert Caballeros Museum for a presentation of her pictures before heading to Reno for an exposition at the Nevada Historical Society.

The Maryland Hunt Cup is America's answer to England's famous Grand National steeplechase. Louise attended, and may have photographed, this annual event in Worthington Valley in the spring of 2002.

She was back in Arizona by May to shoot cowgirls at the Lazy K Bar Guest Ranch nestled in the Tucson Mountains next to Saguaro National Park, one of the few times she photographed western women. "I'm really not a woman's libber," she had confessed to journalist A. J. Flick of the *Tucson Citizen* some years earlier. "I've never been to a woman's rodeo. Isn't that awful?"

She went back to the National Cowgirl Museum and Hall of Fame that June to be present for the opening of the new thirty-three-thousand-square-foot facility in downtown Fort Worth, Texas, and she continued to attend Hall of Fame inductions through the ensuing years.

Louise received the 2002 Tad Lucas award from the Rodeo Historical Society, an arm of Oklahoma City's National Cowboy & Western Heritage Museum. Tad Lucas (1902–90), considered rodeo's First Lady, performed bronc and trick riding for over fifty years. According to the museum, the award is given each year "to women who have exhibited the same sort of extraordinary characteristics [as Lucas] while upholding and promoting our great Western heritage."

Clem McSpadden, who emceed the award program, declared Louise "the Ansel Adams of our sport!"

Louise had watched Tad Lucas perform at Madison Square Garden back in 1945, when she was escaping from Vassar to attend the rodeo in New York City. Never, in her wildest dreams, would she have thought back then that she would receive an award named for the woman who opened so many gates for upcoming rodeo cowgirls.

After a one-woman show at the National Cowgirl Museum and Hall of Fame that ran from November 2003 until February 2004, *Southwest Art*, "the leading magazine devoted to fine art in and of the American West," ran a story about Louise and her work, the first time it had featured a photographer.

The article, "No Guts, No Glory," described Louise as "an unusual combination of feisty and elegant," a description she apparently approved. "Yes, I like that description," she said. "I can pull my tummy in and polish my nails when I have to."

"But," the article continued,

she admits she is most at home in her standard-issue rodeo gear—jeans, boots, and bag balm, a lubricant, on her nails.

In many rodeo events, the dance between cowboy and animal can last just eight seconds, from the time the rider blows out of the chute until he is thrown from the back of the bull or horse. In Serpa's Widow Maker, for example, the horse isn't even out of the chute before the rider is thrown. Her photograph freezes the moment that the cowboy hangs off the horse almost completely vertical in the air. Serpa explains that in this instance she had only a split second to capture the drama on film. "The gate opens, and you start to shoot," she says.

Louise's book tour took her to Farmington, New Mexico; to Fort Worth, Texas; and to almost every sizable city in Arizona, particularly if the town sponsored a rodeo. In 2004 she was part of an Arizona Commission on the Arts traveling exhibit.

Back in Tucson, Pima County recognized her work in January 2005 by inducting her into its Sports Hall of Fame, acknowledging her over forty years of capturing the sweat, determination, entertainment, and spirit of rodeo. At the ceremony she leaned over to rodeo manager Gary Williams and disgustedly remarked, "Do you know the bar has no tequila?" Gary immediately got up and left, returning only when he had acquired a bottle of Jose Cuervo Gold.

Louise would be the first to admit she was slowing down, yet in 2005 the ProRodeo Cowboys Association awarded her the Photographer of the Year belt buckle. Now pushing eighty years of age, she questioned the organization's sanity in presenting her with this trophy. "What on earth for?" she asked. "I only went to one rodeo this year! All they had to say was, 'Well, it's about time.'"

In between roaming over ranches with writer Betty Barr and venturing from one exhibition to another, Louise escaped once again to absorb the richness of Kenya in June 2005, shooting more than fifteen hundred pictures during this trip. By fall she was putting together shows at Phoenix's Sky Harbor Airport and Tucson's Mountain Oyster Club, and an exhibit in Las Vegas, Nevada.

She went to New York in December to attend the launch of Bruce Weber's latest book, *All-American V: Is Love Enough?*, in which he featured Louise in the chapter titled "There's Nothing Like a Dame with a Camera."

In early 2006 the Etherton Gallery ran a monthlong display of her photographs at Tucson's Temple of Music and Art. While she was babysitting this exhibit, she learned she had been selected to serve as grand marshal of the 2006 Tucson Rodeo Parade.

Chapter 27

Nobody has ever gotten a picture of me getting flattened, which really ticks me off.

On February 23, 2006, Louise awoke before dawn, shivering in the chill of an early desert day. Donning her favorite pair of jeans before shoving her head through a black turtleneck, she noted the outdoor thermometer registered below forty degrees; she hoped it would warm considerably before the rodeo parade began around nine o'clock.

Silver was her gem of choice for the parade. She put on round silver earrings, slid an enormous oval silver ring over her finger, and fastened a silver bracelet around her wrist. Even her white hat was trimmed in the glittery precious metal. The hefty silver belt buckle she wrestled around her waist, however, outshone the other jewelry by far. Around her neck she displayed the official grand marshal bolo tie, embellished with an etching of a stagecoach and inscribed with the words *Grand Marshal, 2006*.

Her last piece of attire was a heavy jacket emblazoned with a large "75, Tucson Rodeo" logo, a prized possession she had picked up in 2000 when the rodeo celebrated its seventy-fifth anniversary.

As she made her way through the unlit house, her dog Meggie waited patiently, hoping for a run before dawn. Louise patted the pooch gently before heading out the door into the darkness.

At the fairgrounds she was introduced to those who had braved the morning cold to honor her, gracious in her thanks. "I think [out] of all the things that have happened to me in the last couple of years, this is the biggest award," she said. And she admitted she had never seen the rodeo parade, as she was always busy in the arena, so she was looking forward to seeing it from "the inside out."

She stopped off for an interview with a local radio station that was broadcasting from the rodeo grounds. Acknowledging she usually shot about seven rolls of film for each rodeo, thirty-six exposures each, she also explained how she had to keep track of all the details in these pictures, including the name of every person and animal on the film.

The animal suppliers, Louise said, wanted to buy her pictures of "buck offs," when the rider was displaced from a bucking horse or bull, while cowboys purchased shots that showed them staying on the animals, allowing her to sell pictures from all angles.

By the time she arrived at the start of the parade, the temperature had crept up to forty-two degrees, with the sun having left its secreted spot behind the Santa Catalina Mountains, adding a golden glow to the festivities.

Louise had no intention of riding in a wagon for her big event, the usual mode of transportation for the grand marshal. A magnificent white horse sporting a bright red blanket under its saddle waited patiently for her to mount. She would be the first grand marshal to ride a horse in the parade instead of sitting comfortably in the back of a horse-drawn carriage, even though Louise once admitted, "I ride like a loose sack of grain."

The first to concede that her legs did not work as well these days, she gratefully utilized a stepping stool someone had provided to climb onto the horse. The two-and-a-half-mile parade route started at Park Avenue and Ajo Way before heading south to Irvington Road, then west to Sixth Avenue, ending in a short jaunt north into the rodeo grounds.

Approximately two hundred thousand spectators lined the streets to watch this nonmotorized procession of over 150 floats, wagons, and bands, and Louise must have waved at every one of the bystanders. Cowboys stationed along the route to maintain order and assist with any difficulties that might arise rode out to greet her as she passed by. The horse and wagon she was supposed to ride in dutifully followed behind her, carrying daughters Mia and Lauren along with grandson Taylor.

The grand marshal traditionally completes a turnaround inside the arena to greet the crowd. Louise did ride in the wagon for this leg of the journey, probably because she had grabbed her camera and began taking pictures of the five thousand people who stood and cheered the woman they considered Tucson Rodeo's First Lady.

Age now restricted her workload inside the arena, but Louise still haunted the grounds for the perfect shot and stayed closed to the chutes. "I don't think any 80-year-old belongs out there," she said in a 2005 interview with *Cowboys & Indians* magazine. "A natural diminishing of agility, no matter how great the desire, could lead to the inexcusable—getting in the way of the action."

She focused on a cowboy's hands or his facial expression. She looked for groups of cowboys deep in discussion about the next ride. And she still shot hundreds of images at each event. She claimed she did not have the cleverness to learn digital cameras and left that to younger talent coming up through the ranks of rodeo photography.

Louise at the Tucson Rodeo, circa 1998
COURTESY OF SHARI VAN ALSBURG

"I can record the tension in hands, how the light is acting, how a person is feeling," she said. "It doesn't have to be a cowboy on a horse. As long as it's dedicated movement, I want to capture it."

Even fashion photographer Bruce Weber admitted he learned from Louise's expertise. "Louise had this feeling, which I really like in a photographer, of diving into an empty swimming pool and not knowing where you're going. . . . She had an instinct for believing in what she wanted to show."

He compares her to movie director John Ford, who was one of the first filmographers to put his cameras down on the ground to record the action of a scene.

Louise had no fear of getting her hands dirty, particularly early in her career when she was seeking to improve her craft. "Nobody had that feeling about the way to photograph horses that Louise did," Bruce says. "She had a knack for it."

And although she dodged her share of horses and bulls during the years, she once complained to *American Cowboy* reporter Jesse Mullins, "Nobody has ever gotten a picture of me getting flattened, which really ticks me off."

Tucson artist Barbara Rogers understood what Louise meant when she talked about content and composition in her pictures. After teaching at the University of Arizona from 1990 until 2007, Barbara, now professor emeritus of painting and drawing at the university's School of Art, has exhibited her paintings throughout the world in major galleries.

She met Louise around 2007 and laments, "I wish I had known her longer." The two women talked about the formal issues of their work, and according to Barbara, Louise "was a natural."

Louise "knew about this thing in composition that's a baroqueness, where a form does a turn in space, and when she got that she loved that, and she knew when she got it," Barbara says.

Knowing few artists she could talk with about her photography techniques, Louise relished her meetings with Barbara, which were filled with conversations about content and composition. Many of these discussions commenced and/or concluded at Tucson's Kingfisher Bar & Grill, one of Louise's favorite haunts.

"I think people only talked to her about her content," says Barbara, "not her technical expertise. In art and photography there are three things: subject matter content, technical ability to get the content out on a canvas, and the formal means—how you organize the space you have given yourself to get the content out. One must have all three happening at the same time in order to transcend amateur to a professional level."

It's not easy, according to Barbara. "Photographers have the advantage of making countless attempts at composition because they have that split second and more interest in content, so they can have great content but crappy composition." Louise brought all three elements together when she developed her pictures in the darkroom.

If Louise missed the lighting in a picture, she knew how to "dodge," to bring out the best features of her shot. If the image was a face in the shadows but the rest of the image was in bright sunlight, such as a cowboy on a bucking horse with his hat pulled down tight so he would not lose it, she used dodging to bring out the cowboy's features. Louise might set the exposure of light on the paper for around thirty seconds, and during that time she could use her hands, a piece of cardboard, or even a spoon to block some of the light hitting the cowboy's face so it was not overexposed. By blocking the amount of light in one area, she dodged away light that would darken the area.

For a long time Louise framed her own pictures, but around 1985 she met Beatrice "Bea" Mason, who now owns Lewis Framing Studio in Tucson. The two hit it off immediately, with Bea advising Louise about framing techniques. Eventually, Louise allowed Bea to frame some of her pictures, but according to Bea, she was a very exacting patron.

Bea says Louise once told her that sometime early in her career, and shortly after she had returned from one of her sojourns to Africa or China, Louise met fashion and portrait photographer Richard Avedon while Avedon was in Prescott on a shoot. Almost giddy about meeting such a famous photographer (Avedon is the author of *In the American West*, among many other books), she really wanted his opinion of her work and handed him a selection of pictures she had taken on this recent trip.

Avedon sat down on a rock to review Louise's portfolio, not uttering a word about the content. He rifled through her pictures of wild animals, magnificent flora and fauna, and the faces

Louise found so fascinating on her journeys. Finally he handed her back the pictures and said, "Stick with rodeo." Somewhat taken aback by his abruptness, Louise admitted Richard was probably right.

One day Louise came into Bea's store complaining how tired she was because she had planted a tree that morning. Bea said the temperature that day hovered around 120 degrees but Louise said she had started early, around five in the morning, to dig the hole for the tree. When Bea went to the site, she was stunned to see a gigantic tree almost three stories high, taller than Louise's house, standing proudly in an enormous hole Louise had dug with her own hands. As Bea says, Louise hated to rely on anyone if she could do the job herself.

Chapter 28

I get mad when my knees don't work.

Louise counted among her friends Ruth "Bazy" Tankersley, one of the most prolific Arabian horse breeders in the country. Bazy was publisher of the *Washington Times-Herald* newspaper in Washington, DC, before moving to Tucson in the mid-1970s. An active community leader, she founded Tucson's St. Gregory College Preparatory School, served as president of the board of trustees of the Arizona Sonora Desert Museum, and led the Straw Bale Forum, an organization dedicated to exploring conservation initiatives.

Bazy ran two horse operations in Arizona, the Al-Marah Horse Farm in Tucson and the Hat Ranch near Williams. Louise spent many a day at Bazy's Hat Ranch spread, particularly if she was shooting the Cowpunchers Reunion in Williams, a rodeo made up of working cowboys, ranching families, and those associated with the livestock industry.

Bazy hired Louise to take pictures of her Arabian horses at the Al-Marah Horse Farm. According to Mia, her mother spent a great deal of time shooting, developing the film, and delivering the contact sheets to Bazy. "She knew this could be a big client," says Mia, "and a sizable order. At the end of the week the contact sheets had been returned and they hadn't ordered a thing."

Louise was furious. She stomped around the house, calling Bazy every damnable name she could summon up. After finally expending all her negative energy on condemning Bazy, the horses, and the stable, she called to find out why her pictures were not good enough to purchase. "Louise," said Bazy, "your pictures are wonderful if these were quarter horses. But these are Arabians and they are posed differently. So, if you'd like to set up a time to rephotograph them correctly, let's make another appointment." Louise swallowed her pride and learned how to photograph Arabian horses. "That," according to Mia, "was the beginning of a forty-year friendship."

Another of her close friends was Anheuser-Busch heiress Sallie Wheeler, who lived in Keswick, Virginia. Louise had photographed the Keswick horse show almost every year since 1986. Sallie was considered the grande dame of horse shows, owning and exhibiting top show hunters, Hackney ponies, and American saddlebreds across the country, winning more than two hundred blue ribbons annually. She was also responsible for returning the National Horse Show to Madison Square Garden in 1996 after a seven-year hiatus. The show was considered the pinnacle of black-tie/evening gown affairs in New York society.

Anheuser-Busch sponsored a touring bull-riding event at the National Horse Show, and Sallie invited Louise to be her guest at Madison Square Garden one year, not to photograph the affair but to dress up in her finest and spend the evening with Sallie in her box. According to Tucson Rodeo manager Gary Williams, Louise delighted in telling of Sallie sailing through the hotel lobby every evening to fetch her jewels from the hotel safe.

On one particular night Sallie sported a huge diamond ring that, according to Louise's telling to Gary, was at least three inches long. That evening pop singer Jewel sang the national anthem. Jewel was married to cowboy Ty Murray, a nine-time world champion rodeo cowboy and cofounder and board adviser of the Professional Bull Riders. When she finished her song and headed off the stage, Jewel walked by the box where Sallie and Louise were sitting. Sallie leaned down to shake her hand and tell her what a wonderful performance she had given. Jewel spotted the large diamond ring on Sallie's hand. "Oh my God!" she shouted. "That's the biggest fucking diamond I have ever seen." Sallie let her wear it for the rest of the evening.

Sculptor Malcolm Alexander was a longtime friend with benefits, according to several of Louise's friends. The on-again, off-again romance lasted many years until the handsome Malcolm suddenly up and married without telling Louise. At first Louise was devastated to lose him, but when the union lasted less than a year and he came looking for her to renew their relationship, she found the artist needing too much of her attention and refused to let him back in her life.

Her popularity extended beyond the United States, as evidenced by a young French high school student who read her book *Rodeo* back in 1998. "I picked up a copy of the book (translated into French) when I was in boarding school my sophomore year in high school and read it five or six times," Evan Jayne told a reporter for the *ProRodeo Sports News* in 2008. "I was pretty much obsessed with the book before I came to the U.S. I feel like I almost started a friendship with the guys in the book because I looked at (their pictures) so much."

That year Jayne met the author of the volume he so treasured when he and Louise ran into each other behind the chutes at the Tucson Rodeo.

"He looked at me," she said, "actually jumped off the saddling platform, came over and said he was so glad to meet me. I said, 'You are?' and he said he'd bought my book in French and that's what had made up his mind to become a cowboy.

"It really blew me away."

"I still have the book," Jayne said. "I want to get one here [in English]. I'll get one and keep it with me until I see her again so she can sign it for me."

Bruce Weber often said of Louise, "In her work she was very unselfish. In her friendships she was very unselfish." But if you crossed her, she would delete you from her list of friends forever.

In 2000 Louise began to feel some of the long-term effects from her encounter with the bull that tossed her in the air and pounded her into the ground, over thirty-five years earlier. She told Betty Barr she "couldn't figure out what it was—the clavicle. It started to stick out a little and I thought, must be dying, something's wrong. The doctor said, 'You've got arthritis in the clavicle.' . . . The only other people I know who have arthritis in the clavicle are bull riders!"

"It's hard to keep up with her," Gary Williams told *American Cowboy* in 2006. "You have to sharpen your wits. We get together about once a month and eat peanuts and sip tequila and talk. She calls herself my 'mother superior,' and she really has been like a second mom to me. I can't think of anyone I have any more respect for, personally or professionally."

On October 26, 2006, Gary and his fiancée Rhoda were married in his "mother superior's" backyard. The fifty people who attended were mainly associated with the rodeo, and Louise decided the wedding needed to show respect for the sport. With a pianist Louise hired from the Tucson Symphony Orchestra playing in the background, Gary and Rhoda solemnly recited their vows. As they turned to greet their guests, everyone had donned a clown nose to celebrate the union, courtesy of Louise.

Two days after Gary's wedding, she took off for Morocco, immersing herself in the mystique and majesty of Marrakesh, plus taking several hundred pictures.

Back home she was fitted for hearing aids before opening a show at the Medicine Man Gallery in Tucson, holding an exhibit at the University of Arizona Museum of Art, taking Taylor to see his Aunt Mia in Seattle in the spring of 2007, and heading out with Mia on a cruise to Alaska. That fall she toured Istanbul. At the beginning of this demanding year, as she steadied herself in the Tucson Rodeo arena, she was heard to complain, "I get mad when my knees don't work." She was approaching her eighty-second birthday.

The beginning of 2008 found her putting together a show for the Cowboy & Western Heritage Museum in Oklahoma City that included a display of fifty of her silver gelatin photographic prints, her Tad Lucas award, her ProRodeo Photographer of the Year belt buckle, the bolo tie she wore as grand marshal of the 2006 Tucson Rodeo Parade, and her Nikon N905 camera. Visitors could also see the 2004 interview with Louise and watch the documentary *When the Dust Settles*.

That spring she attended a reunion at her high school alma mater, Garrison Forest School in Baltimore, Maryland, and by fall she was at the Flagstaff Photography Center for the opening of her exhibit *The Rodeo Photography of Louise Serpa*, which ran from September 24 through November 8. "Whether it's bull riding, saddle bronc riding or bareback riding, Louise Serpa has proven that locking horns can be an artform," read the playbill for the exhibit.

The day the Flagstaff exhibit closed, her friend Charlotte Bell opened another showing of her work at the Graham Bell Gallery in Tubac.

During the Flagstaff exhibit Louise felt a little off and did not have her usual spunk. When she returned home she underwent exploratory surgery and received a diagnosis of peritoneal cancer, a malignancy that grows in a thin layer of tissue lining the abdomen. When told the news by doctors at

Reserved sign for Louise at the Tucson Rodeo

COURTESY OF SERPA FAMILY

the University of Arizona Cancer Center, she uttered only a few choice words about her condition. "Oh, shit," was all she had to say.

She started chemotherapy treatments, and just after the beginning of the new year she had another operation. By February 2009 she was up and ready to take her usual spot photographing the Tucson Rodeo.

Since she could not walk as quickly as she once did, she refused to enter the arena; she had not scrambled under a fence, retreating from a charging bull, since 2005. Now she stood on an overturned fifty-five-gallon trash can right next to the gate where horses and bulls exited the arena.

According to Gary Williams, "We built a perch for her, a platform at the same spot, and put her name on it. After she took photos she got down off the trash can and stood on risers behind the chutes."

That year, "the rodeo was almost over," remembers Gary, "but there was a re-ride in the bull riding so another bull was loaded into the chute. Louise contradicted one of her own maxims, 'Never don't pay attention.' The bull came in through the chute where she was standing and hooked her in the leg."

Paramedics were called and it was decided Louise should be transported to a hospital emergency room.

"After the rodeo," says Gary, "there is a critique meeting. Louise was generally in these meetings. She would pour herself a glass of tequila and listen to what was going on, and shoot some candid shots."

Since she was not at the meeting that day, Gary, who had not heard of Louise's accident, assumed she had tired and gone home. When he was told of the bull-goring incident, he immediately called her, not knowing if she was home or still in the hospital. When she picked up the phone, Gary asked, "Where are you?" And she said, "Well, I'm sitting on my back porch drinking tequila, of course." Leg propped up, she was imbibing the only medicine that worked for her.

As Louise had said to Betty Barr back in 2000, "I think there's not one event I haven't been hurt by, not one event."

She constantly amazed Gary with her grit and resilience. "Seeing her come back after her first bout of chemo and come out here and, you know, she had lost all of her hair and she was wearing a scarf with her hat on top of it, and she was just back in her element, and nothing was going to come between her and coming back, absolutely nothing."

The June 2009 page of her calendar noted she was to receive her "last chemo" treatment. But by July she was back in the hospital for a hernia operation and learned the cancer had returned.

The city of Tucson television channel produced the documentary *Cowgirls Don't Cry* in 2009, featuring a beaten-up but not beaten-down Louise. When interviewed for the film at the rodeo grounds, she admitted she was "a little weak in the knees but I'm doing OK."

"I think we ought to get this whole thing settled right now," she said to the camera. Removing her white cowboy hat circled in silver conches, she pulled off the dark skullcap that hugged her bald head, a result of the chemotherapy, and displayed her bravery in the face of death as no one else could, grinning from ear to ear.

As she made her way through the crowd, hands reached out for a handshake or a hug and Louise acknowledged everyone who hailed her. She headed out of the arena steadying herself with a cane in one hand while cradling her camera in the other.

That fall Louise attended the Cowgirl Hall of Fame induction of western sculptor Deborah Copenhaver Fellows, barrel racer Kay Whittaker Young, rancher Cornelia Wadsworth Ritchie, and architect Mary Jane Colter, who has eleven buildings listed on the National Register of Historic Places. Louise's old friend Betty Barr was also at the celebration, and the two ended up together in the hospitality room, where a full bar and extensive array of hors d'oeuvres greeted the attendees.

"Louise took one look at the offering and turned up her nose at what brand of tequila they were offering," recalls Betty. "The next thing we knew, a delivery person arrived with a top-of-the-line tequila just for her, which she and anyone else who wanted it enjoyed for the remainder of the three-day event."

That year Louise also attended the induction into the Cowboy Hall of Fame of her old friend, rodeo clown Chuck Henson. She rarely missed an opportunity to recognize and honor those who had influenced her life's work.

In a 2010 piece in *Zócalo* magazine touting an exhibition of Louise's photographs at the Tucson Botanical Gardens, which "serve as a horticultural center, a sanctuary for wild birds, and as a center for education," the reporter described eighty-four-year-old Louise's eyes as sharply focused, with "a fire that burns behind them, conveying the wisdom of a fully lived life that she has also beautifully captured on film."

The Botanical Gardens exhibit included not only Louise's images—this time of African wildlife instead of her rodeo shots—but also the contemporary photographs of her daughter Mia, only the second time Mia had shown her work. And even though her mother still had the seat of honor at the Tucson Rodeo, Mia was now its official photographer.

When interviewed for the *Zócalo* article, Mia proudly remarked, "It is a great honor and privilege for me to continue the work and pictures she has provided for nearly forty-five years."

The reception for the exhibit was held three days after the rodeo started, but Louise was on hand at the Gardens to sing for the audience who had come to admire her art. It was the last time she sang in public.

Even cancer, however, could not slow Louise for long. She was off to Bruce Weber's place in Montana that summer, feeling so good she thought the cancer was gone again.

Most of the time Louise slept in a teepee on Bruce's ranch, and rode with whoever wanted to saddle up and go with her. Of course there was always music—she sang to the mountains, to the horses, and to anyone who would listen. She came, according to Bruce (who admits Louise was like an older sister to him), because the food was great and the tequila even better.

Louise rarely missed the VIP barn dance that the Tucson Rodeo holds every year after the action has subsided, and cancer certainly did not deter her attendance. The toast of the ball for the last few years of her life, she was roundly roasted by a bevy of cowboys and Arizona celebrities. She had no hair and kept her cane close by, yet the gathering of men standing in line to talk to her wound around the ballroom. So commanding was her presence even under debilitating physical conditions that no other woman could compete with her for the limelight.

One day Barbara Rogers met Louise at Tucson's Kingfisher Bar & Grill after she had started chemotherapy treatment. Louise arrived before Barbara, and by the time Barbara got there, "Louise was with a cute young man. With chemo, stress of cancer, with cap on, she still looked vibrant and gorgeous. Still sending off these vibes, completely feminine."

On October 7, 2010, Louise wrote a short note on her calendar: "cancer back."

Chapter 29

I've had a good life.

Bruce Weber had not seen Louise in a while. He knew she was in the battle of her life and thought it best not to interfere with her and her family during this time. When he finally heard from her, he was so elated he went out and bought her a slew of Christmas gifts. When she called to thank him, he said her phone call was the best gift he received that year.

She told Bruce she had had a reprieve from the cancer. She was working on an exhibition and making plans for a trip to Hawaii.

"I'm going to beat this," she told Bruce. "I've had a good life, did well, taken some pictures I'm proud of and I've had a lot of fun."

By January, as she was making plans to go to Hawaii, the *American Quarter Horse Journal* published an interview in which Louise adamantly said photography was "the greatest passport to the world."

Off she flew to Hawaii but returned just before the opening of the 2011 Tucson Rodeo. She desperately wanted to stick around long enough to shoot the 2012 competition, which would have been her fiftieth, but this would be her last show.

On March 29 she spoke at Tucson's Adobe Corral, a local chapter of the history club Westerners International, about her years of photographing rodeos from one end of Arizona to the other. On April 9 she was in the hospital with heart problems. Back on chemotherapy, she had lymph nodes removed, her white count dropped, and her legs pained her terribly. Again in the hospital that September, time was running out.

She rallied enough to attend one of Taylor's basketball games with Lauren before mother and daughter headed back to Louise's home.

"I asked her if I could see some of our photo albums from when we were growing up because I needed to get some pictures for something I was working on for her birthday," Lauren remembers.

"We hadn't opened up the albums in years. As I went through them, I would find pictures that would trigger memories in both of us, and that fifteen minutes turned into three hours of reminiscing about our lives together and realizing how blessed we were. When I was leaving the house, Mom said, 'Thanks, I needed that.'"

"I started to tear up and didn't want Mom to see me cry, so I walked away." Her mother called her back, and Lauren faced her with tears streaming down her face.

"Everything is going to be OK," Louise told her daughter.

"I just looked at her, and she was so beautiful," Lauren says. "For a moment I forgot she was sick."

Louise had already donated her rodeo photographs and memorabilia to the National Cowboy & Western Heritage Museum. According to Mia, "The day all her negatives were packed up in a van, headed to Oklahoma City, my mother went into the hospital one last time. But before she left [for the hospital], she actually took a picture of the van fully packed, complete with license plate."

The last entry written by Louise on her calendar, dated December 2, 2011, was for a social occasion at the Mountain Oyster Club. She did not attend.

On December 7, 2011, Mia wrote on her mother's calendar, "Mom home. Hospice begins," concluding almost fifty years of recording the life history of Louise Serpa.

The hospice program provides care to patients who are in the final stages of their life. Patients and their families receive understanding and compassion as they transition from this world into the next phase of their otherworldly existence. The organization "affirms life and regards dying as a normal process." Care is provided either at home or in a homelike setting. Louise chose to remain in the home she had built, designed, and lived in for the last fifteen years.

People came in droves to pay their last respects to the lady who had influenced so many of their lives through her photography and her graciousness. She had a hospital bed placed in the front room of her house and would hold court as flowers and balloons arrived hourly. People stopped by bearing smiles while holding back tears. Everyone was invited to have a drink with her.

Brenda Griffin worked in the press trailer on the Tucson Rodeo grounds and met Louise in 1997. "When she walked through the rodeo grounds, she spoke to everyone," Brenda says. "She was the first person I ever met who had a guest book at her house. And when you went there you signed the guest book. It didn't matter if you went there every day."

Christmas 2011 was difficult for everyone. Brenda was there when singer/songwriter Jenny Yates brought her guitar and sang songs around Louise's hospital bed. "I cried all the way home in my car because I thought that was the last time I would see her," Brenda says of Louise. And yet, "Being with her and watching her die was an incredible life lesson. She was not afraid to die. She would not allow anyone to be sad."

Jenny had known Louise for several years and had made a film for her, *The Day Louise Led the Parade, February 23, 2006*, when Louise was grand marshal of the Tucson Rodeo Parade. "It was a gift for her," says Jenny, "a remembrance of the day."

Gary Williams showed up often those last few days, just to sit and chat with his old drinking buddy. On one of these occasions, she asked him how long they had been sparring back and forth, and Gary realized it had been over thirty years. "Damn, that's not long enough," Louise said. "So I guess I'll stick around a bit longer."

Tequila still eased her pain more than any prescribed medication. Louise constantly asked for a double shot. "Chemo no longer works," she told a reporter for an *Inside Tucson Business* article. "When I need relief, I pour myself a shot of tequila."

Around ten o'clock one morning about a week before she died, Louise looked at Gary and muttered, "You know I don't like to drink alone." Gary tried to persuade her to wait a while. "Well, it's a little early," he said. Louise repeated herself. "You know I don't like to drink alone." So Gary got up and went to the bar to make drinks for Louise, Mia, and himself. He and Mia sat on either side of Louise's bed discussing mundane issues as Louise's eyes slowly closed. Suddenly her eyes popped open and she blurted out to her two rather boring companions, "You know, you two are full of shit." Everyone in the room burst out laughing, some chuckling through their tears.

During those last days everyone tried their best to remain cheerful around the woman who had no tears for her own plight. Even when she could not open her eyes she was the consummate photographer, holding up imaginary negatives to the light, trying to ensure she had just the right amount of exposure to create the perfect image.

On January 5, 2012, at eight thirty in the morning, Louise died. "Malignant Neoplasm Peritoneum" is listed as the cause on her death certificate.

Louise was a dominant figure at rodeos for over fifty years, lugging heavy cameras and equipment across fields of dirt and grime. She was the personification of grace under pressure, and her love of rodeo stimulated its popularity through her photographs.

Her obituary appeared in numerous publications, including the *New York Times*, which described her as "elegant, but dainty; classy, but not snobbish. She would come adorned with jewelry and leave covered in dirt. She dressed like a lady and drank with the boys. She stuck out and fit in."

According to the *Arizona Daily Star* obituary, "Louise will be remembered most for her incredible generosity, endearing interest in others, her uncanny ability to speak her mind and a strong spirit to laugh and sing louder than anyone."

"Louise didn't hesitate to get down in the arena dirt on a knee or two when that's what it took," said Kendra Santos in the *ProRodeo Sports News* article about Louise's death. "She fought to make the most of every frame, and chronicled four generations of rodeo people, from junior rodeo ranks to the best in the world. Louise shared the love of the game and competitive spirits of the cowboys she captured on film."

"We always thought she would be there," said Gary Williams.

Louise Serpa opened doors for women in photography with the click of her shutter. Her spirit continues to soar over the rodeo arena as she keeps an eye on youngsters coming up through the ranks to shoot some of the most dramatic and dangerous pictures of their lives. One of them might feel a gentle breeze as Louise pushes them out of the way of a charging steer or bronc. They might even hear her words of admonishment—"Never don't pay attention."

Epilogue

The 2012 Tucson Rodeo exceeded expectations, according to rodeo manager Gary Williams. The weather cooperated and ticket sales skyrocketed. "We all thought that Louise was up there pulling strings for us. Every day after the rodeo, we poured a shot of tequila and left it on the bar for her."

Louise Serpa was eighty-six years old when she died on January 5, 2012. The rodeo grounds were silent that day, but a few weeks later, hundreds came to pay their respects to the woman they had admired and accepted as part of their rodeo family. Cowboys she had photographed years before, along with their sons and grandsons, whom she also had photographed throughout her extensive career, attended the wake. All had experienced her charismatic presence as they bounded out of the chute and landed with a thud on the hard arena floor only to hear her shutter clicking away, memorializing an outstanding ride or the agony of a bad fall.

For the wake, her daughter Lauren put together a photographic retrospective of her mother that flashed across a large screen. With each new picture someone had a memory to share. At the end of an evening filled with reminiscences, songs, good food, and libations, the crowd gave one last rousing tequila toast to the photographer, and the woman, who had meant so much to them throughout their careers.

Louise donated her vast collection of rodeo photographs and memorabilia to the National Cowboy & Western Heritage Museum so they would be available for anyone to view. Chuck Schroeder, who was executive director of the museum for over ten years, was quoted in Louise's *New York Times* obituary. "There have been a number of notable rodeo photographers and they each had their unique style. Hers was certainly the most artful of any that had ever been."

"Did the rodeo capture Louise," he asked, "or did Louise capture the rodeo?"

The tall, poised, strong, and strikingly beautiful Louise is remembered by her two daughters as a loving but often absent mother, yet they also know she gave them all she could while trying to provide for them the best way she knew how. Says daughter Mia:

> *When we went with her to the rodeos, my sister and I were on our own because our mother was in the arena working from the moment the action started.*
>
> *My mother used to tell me to "cowboy up" and then later tell me to act more like a lady. I used to be so confused by that, but all you had to do was look at her. She was always able to accomplish both.*
>
> *Every day when I returned home from school I would enter the house and hear my mother's voice singing to the radio from within her darkroom closet. I learned at an early age not to open the door, thereby ruining the photographic paper by getting it exposed to natural light. I would yell "I'm home" and wait for the sound of the paper chamber closing and my mother's reply, "I'll be right out."*

Lauren remembers advice Louise gave her years ago, after she had dissolved a two-year romance. Her mother said the young man was not right for her because he did not pass the test.

"What test?" Lauren asked.

Her mother told her to think of circumstances and situations that meant the most to her—family gatherings, important people in her life, individuals she admired—and imagine taking her boyfriend to these places and meeting these people. "If you don't feel comfortable introducing him or you can't imagine him there, then he is not the right person for you."

"Don't worry," she told her concerned daughter, "your Prince Charming is out there."

She had frank advice for others too. "Don't get too big for your britches, and don't believe your own bull . . ." she told cowboy Joe Parsons when he became a member of the PRCA Board. In a *ProRodeo Sports News* article about Louise's death, Parsons remembered: "She'd known me since I was a kid, so she was talking to me like a mentor or a grandpa would. She reminded me that none of us is ever too good to listen. When I was young, I was a typical cowboy who thought cowboys were the only stars of the show. Louise was the one who made me understand that everybody who works at the rodeo is part of the sport and important to its success. She sure made a lasting impression."

Louise's fondness for tequila, preferably Jose Cuervo Gold, was known throughout the rodeo industry. A reporter for the *American Quarter Horse Journal* who interviewed Louise in 2011 remarked, "When Louise Serpa greets you late in the afternoon in the driveway of her adobe home in Tucson, Arizona, she'll probably offer you a tequila and tonic. It's her brand of English tea."

"Photography has taught her to watch, wait and be ready to capture the moment when you can. So say 'yes' to the tequila and tonic, if she offers. And have your camera ready."

"I don't want people to forget her," says Bruce Weber. "I think she will be an inspiration to photographers of all kinds, to see her pictures, to see their beauty.

"If she was alive today, I would say to her, 'Hey, Louise, I'm going to meet you up in Montana in the spring when all the trees are coming out in bloom, like late spring or early summer, and we're just going to take a road trip.'"

Louise was always gracious in recognizing those who influenced and enhanced her life. As she acknowledged in her book *Rodeo*, she appreciated "the countless hard-core rodeo families who have nurtured and protected me in the arena, bought my photographs, fed me, housed me, teased me, and generally kept me going through three generations. I could not have persevered or survived without you."

Louise left a heritage of amazing images, pictures that tell the story of rodeo, the power and the prowess of animals as engaged in the sport as is the cowboy. If future rodeo photographers learn anything from her determination and expertise behind the camera, they will enter the arena with wary confidence, one eye on the animal charging across the arena, and the other glued to the camera. They will have to be quick on their feet and not afraid to get more than a little dirty as they dodge for safety. And before the dust settles, they will remember the woman who showed them how to take a still photograph and turn it into a picture that comes to life in the quiet, lonely obscurity of a darkroom closet.

Bibliography

Published Sources

Ault, Louise Larocque. "Bit Free Space." *The Chapin School Alumnae Bulletin*, 1988, 2–3.

Barker, Scott. "Rodeos to Rossini: Louise Serpa's Home Rounds Up Her Many Passions." *Tucson Lifestyle*, February 2005.

Barr, Betty. "Louise Serpa, Rodeo Photographer." *Sonoita Weekly Bulletin*, September 5, 2001.

De Landri, Carla. "More Rodeo Days." *Vassar Quarterly*, Spring 1995.

Doggert, Janet. "Getting Close to the Action." *Taylor Talk*, Winter 1998.

Duarte, Carmen. "Rodeo Photographer Far from Negative." *Arizona Daily Star*, March 4, 1984.

Ehrenstrom, Art. "Vassar Girl Risks Ribs, Lens." *Arizona Daily Star*, July 16, 1967.

Fimbres, Gabrielle. "Riding Her Dream." *Tucson Citizen*, February 19, 2005.

Flick, A. J. "First Out for the Shoot." *Tucson Citizen*, June 7, 1997.

Gangelhoff, Bonnie. "No Guts, No Glory." *Southwest Art* 33 (May 2004).

Hamilton, Christine. "Dust and Light." *American Quarter Horse Journal*, January 2011.

Haynes, Kevin. "Western Exposure." *Mercedes Momentum*, Winter 1998.

Hutchings, David. "In the Art of Catching Rodeo Action on Film, No One Stands Taller Than Louise Serpa." *People*, October 3, 1983.

"In the Eye of the Hurricane." *Pro Rodeo Sports News*, February 22, 1984, and March 7, 1984.

Laird, Cheryl. "Eye of Action: Louise Serpa Zooms In on Rough-Ridin' World of Rodeo." *Houston Chronicle*, November 24, 1994.

"Lex Connelly Killed in Airplane Crash." *ProRodeo Sports News*, April 18, 1984.

"Louise Serpa" (obituary notice). *Arizona Daily Star*, January 9, 2012.

"Louise Serpa Joins Generations Table." *Empire Ranch Foundation News* 3, no. 3 (August 2002).

Lowe, Charlotte. "Serpa's 'Rodeo' Ropes You In." *Tucson Citizen*, December 29, 1994.

Manser, Jami. "Poignant Vision." *Zócalo*, January 28, 2010.

Morris, Michael. *The Cowboy Life*. New York: Simon & Schuster, 1993.

Mullins, Jesse, Jr. "An Eye for What Counts." *American Cowboy*, July/August 2006.

Partain, Kyle. "Cowgirl Hall Tabs Serpa for Honor." *ProRodeo Sports News*, October 6, 1999.

Patterson, Randall. "An Eye on the Chute." *The Houston Post*, November 3, 1994.

"Photographer Louise Serpa and Her Artistic Life in the Rodeo Ring." *Inside Tucson Business*, January 6, 2012.

"Photography." *The New Yorker*, August 3, 1992, 17 (Column was written by Ingrid Seshi).

Regan, Margaret. "Art of the Artist: Two Exhibits at the Gallery of the Sun Show Not-Oft-Depicted Sides of Ted DeGrazia." *Tucson Weekly*, September 13, 2012.

———. "The Decisive Moment: Louise Serpa's Photographs Show the Allure of the Fading Old West." *Tucson Weekly*, February 11, 2005.

Sachar, Emily. "Louise Serpa: Her Legendary Rodeo Photography and Long Life of Locking Horns with Camera in Hand." *Cowboys & Indians* 13, no. 8 (December 2005).

Santos, Kendra. "Serpa Leaves an Iconic Image." *ProRodeo Sports News*, January 20, 2012.

Seberger, Will. "Rodeo Photographer, Western Legend Louise Serpa Dead at 86." TucsonSentinel.com, January 5, 2012. www.tucsonsentinel.com/arts/report/010512_serpa_obit/rodeo-photographer-western-legend-louise-serpa-dead-86. Accessed March 18, 2015.

Serpa, Louise L. *Rodeo*. New York: Aperture Foundation, 1994.

Sheridan, Thomas E. *Arizona: A History*. Tucson: University of Arizona Press, 1995.

Simpson, Corky. "Photog Still Thinks Rodeo's a Snap." *Tucson Citizen*, February 23, 1999.

Skinner, M. Scott. "Pioneer Rodeo Photographer Honored." *Arizona Daily Star*, November 2, 1999.

Sonnichsen, C. L. *Tucson: The Life and Times of an American City*. Norman: University of Oklahoma Press, 1987.

Stearns, Rhoda Sedgwick. "1999 National Cowgirl Hall of Fame Honorees." *Fort Worth Business Press*, October 22, 1999.

Steverson, Ed. "Easterner Doffed her Gloves to Become Top Rodeo Photographer." *Arizona Daily Star*, May 3, 1996.

Vance, Susan. "DeGrazia Gallery to Host Reception Friday." *Arizona Daily Star*, January 19, 2012.

Vanderpool, Tim. "Louise in the Dust." *Western Horseman*, June 1994.

———. "Rodeo's Grande Dame." *Arizona Highways* 83, no. 11 (November 2007).

White, Kristen M. "Source of Inspiration." *ProRodeo Sports News*, April 25, 2008.

Wikins, Emily, "Sweetheart of the Rodeo." *New York Times*, January 12, 2012.

Woerner, Gail Hughbanks. "Rodeo Historical Society Inducts Honorees." www.rodeoattitude.com/dir_hd/gail/past_6htm. Accessed May 29, 2012.

Wooden, Wayne S., and Gavin Ehringer. *Rodeo in America*. Lawrence: University Press of Kansas, 1996.

Younger, Jamar. "Louise Serpa, Photographer. Her Work Revealed Art of Rodeo Action." *Arizona Daily Star*, January 9, 2012.

Unpublished Sources

Journal of Louise's trip to Africa in 1990. Serpa family papers.

Journal of Louise's trip to England and Ireland with her daughters in 1972. Serpa family papers.

Letters from Lex Connelly to Louise Larocque, 1943–1946. Serpa family papers.

Louise Serpa calendars dating from 1963 through 2011. Serpa family papers.

Interviews

Barr, Betty. Interview by author. Tucson, Arizona, June 13, 2012.

Bell, Charlotte. Interview by author. Tubac, Arizona, September 28, 2012.

Browne, Anne Curtis. Telephone interview by author. June 4, 2012.

Donoghue, Wendy. Telephone interviews by author. June 4, 2012, and June 6, 2013.

Glasston, Hannah. Email correspondence. September 14, 2012.

Goodman, John K. "Jack" and Aline. Interview by author. Tucson, Arizona, September 26, 2012.

Grammar, Taylor. Interview by author. Tucson, Arizona, June 7, 2013.

Griffin, Brenda. Telephone interview by author. May 15, 2013.

Harris, Melissa. Telephone interview by author. February 4, 2014.

Henson, Chuck and Nancy. Interview by author. Oro Valley, Arizona, July 4, 2013.

Larocque, Mia. Interview by author. Tucson, Arizona, May 2, 2012 (initial interview; others followed).

Lynch, Marty. Interview by author. Tucson, Arizona, November 5, 2013.

Mason, Beatrice. Interview by author. Tucson, Arizona, January 15, 2014.

Rogers, Barbara. Telephone interview by author. January 18, 2014.

Serpa, Lauren. Interview by author. Tucson, Arizona, May 7, 2012 (initial interview; others followed).

Smith, Eleanor. Telephone interview by author. July 27, 2013.

Weber, Bruce. Telephone interview by author. January 28, 2014.

Wheelwright, Mary. Telephone interview by author. June 25, 2012.

Williams, Gary. Interview by author. Tucson, Arizona, September 22, 2012.

Yates, Jenny. Email interview by author. May 2013.

Audio/Video Sources

Cowgirls Don't Cry. DVD. Jennifer McKinney, writer/producer. Dan Sheffer, photojournalist. City of Tucson Cable Channel 12. July 2009.

The Day Louise Led the Parade. Personal video. Jenny Yates, producer. February 23, 2006.

National Cowgirl Museum Hall of Fame induction. VHS. October 28, 1999.

New York Life Insurance Co. *The Wagons West and On to Oregon Cavalcade Wagon Train of 1959*. DVD. Jean Van Meter, filmmaker. Independence, Oregon, 1959.

"Remembering Louise Serpa." KVOA *Tucson Today*, February 24, 2012.

Serpa, Louise. Interview by Michael Boyle. *Arizona Illustrated*. PBS documentary. VHS. Tucson, Arizona, January 10, 1995.

Serpa, Louise. Interview by Jim Campbell. *The Horseman's Rodeo Weekly* radio show, 2004.

Serpa, Louise. Interview by Leonard Lopate. "New York & Co." *Radio Talk TV on WYNC*. VHS. Produced by Members of WNYC, November 1994.

Serpa, Louise. Interview by Chuck Rand for Rodeo Historical Society Oral History Project. DVD. Dickinson Research Center, National Cowboy & Western Heritage Museum, Oklahoma City, Oklahoma, March 31, 2004.

Serpa, Louise interview. *Voices of Tucson*. City of Tucson Cable Channel 12, January 4, 1995.

To Tell the Truth. VHS, September 1, 1967. Private collection of Serpa family.

Tucson Rodeo. "Louise Serpa Tribute." YouTube video, 3:14. February 25, 2012. www.youtube.com/watch?v=u8gkJYTuyRg&feature=player_ embedded.

When the Dust Settles. VHS. PBS. Dan Duncan, director. 1995.

Internet Sources

Hansen, Eric. "Not Clowning Around." *American Cowboy*. www.american-cowboy.com/culture/not-clowning-around. Accessed June 6, 2013.

McDonald, Joann. "Louise L. Serpa. The Ballsiest Lady I Ever Knew." www.writeontruth819.wordpress.com/2012/01/07/louise-serpa-the-ballsiest-lady-i-ever-knew. Accessed January 10, 2012.

"Sammy's Bowery Follies: Revisiting the Old 'Alcoholic Haven.'" *Life* magazine 17, no. 23 (December 4, 1944), 57–60. http://gothamist .com/2013/01/04/sammys_bowery_follies.php#photo-1. Accessed August 13, 2013.

Index

About the Author

Jan Cleere is an award-winning author of four historical nonfiction books, three of them published by TwoDot. *More Than Petticoats: Remarkable Nevada Women* was a 2006 finalist for the Women Writing the West WILLA award. The Nevada Women's History Project elected Cleere to its Roll of Honor for her work on Nevada women's history.

CHRIS RICHARDS PHOTOGRAPHY

Outlaw Tales of Arizona was recognized nationally as the winner of the 2007 National Federation of Press Women's literary competition for historical nonfiction. *Amazing Girls of Arizona: True Stories of Young Pioneers* was named one of the best books of 2009 by the Arizona Book Publishers Association and awarded best young adult nonfiction by the same organization. *Levi's & Lace: Arizona Women Who Made History* (Rio Nuevo Publishers) received recognition from the 2012 Arizona/New Mexico Book Publishers Association. Cleere also writes a monthly column for Tucson's *Arizona Daily Star* newspaper, "Western Women," detailing the lives of early Arizona pioneers. She lives in Oro Valley, Arizona.